my revision notes

OCR AS/A-level History

THE COLD WAR IN EUROPE

1941–1995

Nicholas Fellows
Mike Wells

HODDER
EDUCATION
AN HACHETTE UK COMPANY

Orders: please contact Bookpoint Ltd, 130 Milton Park, Abingdon, Oxon OX14 4SE. Telephone: +44 (0)1235 827720. Fax: +44 (0)1235 400401. Email education@bookpoint.co.uk Lines are open from 9 a.m. to 5 p.m., Monday to Saturday, with a 24-hour message answering service. You can also order through our website: www.hoddereducation.co.uk

ISBN: 978 1 5104 1642 0

© Nicholas Fellows, Mike Wells 2018

First published in 2018 by
Hodder Education,
An Hachette UK Company
Carmelite House
50 Victoria Embankment
London EC4Y 0DZ

www.hoddereducation.co.uk

Impression number 10 9 8 7 6 5 4 3 2

Year   2022   2021   2020   2019   2018

Cover photo © OlegDoroshin – stock.adobe.com
Illustrations by Integra
Typeset in India by Integra Software Services
Printed in Spain

A catalogue record for this title is available from the British Library.

My revision planner

4 The end of the Cold War 1984–1995

REVISED

Introduction

Unit 2: Non-British period study

Component 2 involves the study of a period of non-British history, and at AS-level will also involve the evaluation of a historical interpretation from one of two named topics. The type of essay set for both AS and A-level is similar, but the AS mark scheme does not have a Level 6 (see page 7).

The Cold War in Europe 1941–1995

The specification lists the contents under four Key Topics:
- Key Topic 1 – The origins of the Cold War to 1945
- Key Topic 2 – The development of the Cold War 1946–1955
- Key Topic 3 – The Cold War 1956–1984
- Key Topic 4 – The end of the Cold War 1984–1995

Although each period of study is set out in chronological sections in the specification, an exam question may arise from one or more of these sections.

AS-level

The AS examination includes all the content.
- Section A: you are required to answer **one** question from a choice of **two**. These will be traditional essays and will require you to use your knowledge to explain, analyse and assess key features of the period studied and then to reach a judgement about the issue in the question. The question is worth 30 marks.
- Section B: you are required to answer **one** interpretation question. The specification names the two Key Topics from which the interpretation will be drawn. Questions will require you to evaluate, in the form of either one or two sentences, the strengths and limitations of a given historical interpretation. You do this by applying your own knowledge and awareness of the debate to the given interpretation. The question is worth 20 marks.

The exam will last one and a half hours, and you are advised to spend slightly more time on Section A.

At AS, Unit 2 will be worth a total of 50 marks and 50 per cent of your AS.

A-level

The A-level examination at the end of the course includes all the content. You are required to answer **one** question with **two** parts from a choice of **two** questions.
- Each question will have **two** parts. Question (a) will be a short essay in which you are asked to analyse two issues and reach a judgement as to which is the more important or significant. Question (b) is a traditional period study essay and will require you to use your knowledge to explain, analyse and assess key features of the period studied and then to reach a judgement about the issue in the question.
- The short essay is worth 10 marks and the traditional essay is worth 20 marks.
- The two parts of each question will be drawn from different areas of the specification.

The exam will last for one hour. You should spend about 20 minutes on Question (a) and 40 minutes on Question (b).

At A-level, Unit 2 will be worth a total of 30 marks and 15 per cent of your A-level.

In both the AS and A-level examinations, you are being tested on:
- your ability to use relevant historical information
- your skill in analysing factors and reaching a judgement.

In the AS examination you are also being tested on your ability to analyse and evaluate the different ways in which aspects of the past have been interpreted.

How to use this book

This book has been designed to help you develop the knowledge and skills necessary to succeed in the examination.

- The book is divided into four sections – one for each section of the AS and A-level specifications.
- Each section is made up of a series of topics, organised into double-page spreads.
- On the left-hand page, you will find a summary of the key content you need to learn.
- Words in bold in the key content are defined in the glossary (see page 86).
- On the right-hand page, you will find exam-focused activities.

Together, these two strands of the book will provide you with the knowledge and skills essential for examination success.

▼ **Key historical content**

▼ **Exam-focused activities**

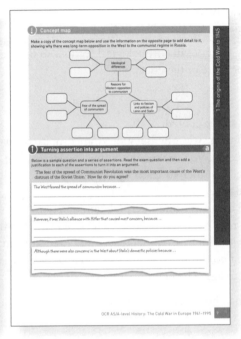

Examination activities

There are three levels of exam-focused activities:

- Band 1 activities are designed to develop the foundation skills needed to pass the exam. These have a green heading and this symbol:
- Band 2 activities are designed to build on the skills developed in Band 1 activities and to help you to achieve a C grade. These have an orange heading and this symbol:
- Band 3 activities are designed to enable you to access the highest grades. These have a purple heading and this symbol:

Some of the activities have answers or suggested answers, which can be found on pages 91–96. These have the following symbol to indicate this:

Each section ends with exam-style questions and sample answers with an examiner's commentary. This will give you guidance on what is expected in order to achieve the top grade.

You can also keep track of your revision by ticking off each topic heading in the book, or by ticking the checklist on the contents page. Tick each box when you have:

- revised and understood the topic
- completed the activities.

Mark schemes

For some of the activities in the book it will be useful to refer to the mark schemes for this paper. These have been abbreviated below.

AS-level

Level	Essay	Interpretation
5	Mostly focused, supported answer with good analysis and evaluation to reach a supported judgement. **25–30**	Very good analysis of the interpretation, aware of the debate and use of detailed knowledge to evaluate the strengths and limitations. **17–20**
4	Some focus with support, analysis with limited evaluation and judgement. **19–24**	Good analysis of the interpretation, some awareness of the debate and use of knowledge to evaluate the strengths and limitations. **13–16**
3	Partial focus on the question, with some knowledge and analysis, but little or no judgement. **13–18**	Partial analysis of the interpretation, some knowledge and awareness of the debate. May be limited in treatment of strength or limitations. **9–12**
2	Focus is descriptive and may be more on the topic generally than on the question asked. Any analysis may be implied. **7–12**	Limited analysis, may describe the interpretation and the debate. Any evaluation is implied or superficial. **5–8**
1	Focus on the topic and attempts at analysis will be little more than assertion. **1–6**	Focused more on the topic generally than on the given interpretation. Knowledge is general and evaluation is asserted. **1–4**

A-level

Level	Short-answer essay	Essay
6	Analyses and evaluates both factors with detailed knowledge to reach a developed judgement. **9–10**	Well focused, supported answer with very good analysis and developed evaluation to reach a supported and sustained judgement. **17–20**
5	Analyses and evaluates both factors with some knowledge to reach a developed judgement. **7–8**	Mostly focused, supported answer with good analysis and evaluation to reach a supported judgement. **13–16**
4	Some analysis and evaluation of both factors, with some support and judgement. **5–6**	Some focus with support, analysis with limited evaluation and judgement. **10–12**
3	Partial analysis and evaluation with some knowledge to reach a basic judgement. **3–4**	Partial focus on the question, with some knowledge and analysis, but little or no judgement. **7–9**
2	Limited analysis and knowledge, with a simple judgement. **2**	Focus is descriptive and may be more on the topic generally than on the question asked. Any analysis may be implied. **4–6**
1	General analysis and knowledge with assertion. **1**	Focus on the topic and attempts at analysis will be little more than assertion. **1–3**

1 The origins of the Cold War to 1945

The situation in 1941, ideological differences and attitudes

Ideological differences and attitudes

The **Bolshevik Revolution** in Russia in October 1917 led to a civil war between the 'reds' and their opponents the 'whites'. The decision of the new revolutionary government to seek peace alienated Russia's allies: Britain, the USA, France and Japan. These powers were hostile to the aims and ideology of the new Russian regime led by Vladimir Lenin. The Russian Civil War created a lot of bitterness and the new **Union of Soviet Socialist Republics** was deeply divided from the Western powers.

Ideology

Lenin and the Bolsheviks were inspired by **Karl Marx** (1818–83), who believed that the more advanced industrial countries were bound to experience revolution and that the collapse of the capitalist system was inevitable. Just as the new industrial middle class had replaced the aristocracy, so they in turn would be replaced by the industrial workers (**proletariat**). First a working-class dictatorship would be established; then the state would wither away and there would be a community of equals, an ideal classless society.

Capitalism versus communism

Marx saw capitalism as a system of exploitation. Money was invested in businesses (capital). This meant that bosses and investors needed profits in order to invest more money to make more profits. This was possible only by exploiting workers, and it resulted in a pointless pursuit of money for its own sake and in deep social and economic inequality. It also created political inequality as the rich dominated politics. Defenders of capitalism pointed out that invested money created jobs, social and economic opportunities, prosperity and healthy competition, which helped consumers. They also linked the economic freedom to invest, set up businesses and make money with political freedom.

Opposition

Western powers continued to see Communist Russia as an enemy. They had been shocked by the murder of the Tsar and his family, and by the Bolshevik hopes of world revolution promoted by the **Comintern**, an international organisation to promote Communism.

The interwar years

The rise of **fascism** in Germany and Italy led to a big political divide in Europe.

The USSR remained isolated. **Stalin** pursued dramatic industrialisation policies accompanied by severe repression of the Russian people and purges of the Communist party. This seemed dangerous to many in the West.

Stalin's attempt to unite all left-wing groups against Nazism by creating a **Popular Front** only served to worry conservative opinion. His support for the Spanish Communists during a Civil War in Spain (1936–39) also led to fears. Driven by a need to protect the USSR, Stalin signed a pact with Hitler in August 1939. This seemed to show that communism had more in common with fascism than democracy.

The situation by 1941

When World War II broke out in 1939, Stalin regained lost lands in the Baltic states and Poland, which were subjected to a tyrannous repression. The West sympathised with Finland, which resisted occupation in the Winter War of 1939–40. Indeed, Britain seriously contemplated declaring war on both the USSR and Germany.

By 1941 the hostility between the USSR and the West was well established:
- There were deep ideological differences.
- The West feared Russian influence.
- The USSR resented its exclusion from the diplomacy of the 1930s.
- The West despised the Nazi–Soviet Pact and Russian expansion in Eastern Europe.

! Concept map

Make a copy of the concept map below and use the information on the opposite page to add detail to it, showing why there was long-term opposition in the West to the communist regime in Russia.

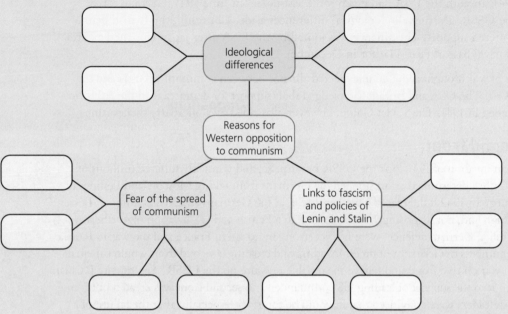

i Turning assertion into argument ⓐ

Below is a sample question and a series of assertions. Read the exam question and then add a justification to each of the assertions to turn it into an argument.

'The fear of the spread of Communist Revolution was the most important cause of the West's distrust of the Soviet Union.' How far do you agree?

The West feared the spread of communism because...

_____

_____

However, it was Stalin's alliance with Hitler that caused most concern, because...

_____

_____

Although there were also concerns in the West about Stalin's domestic policies because...

_____

_____

Wartime tensions in the Grand Alliance

The Grand Alliance comprised Britain, the USA and the USSR, against the so-called Axis powers: Germany, Italy and Japan. Britain had stood alone against Germany and Italy from 1940 to 1941, though the USA had given some assistance. In June 1941, German forces invaded the USSR. Putting all ideological differences aside, **Churchill**, the British prime minister, offered support. The alliance was joined by the USA after Japan launched an attack on the US naval base at Pearl Harbor in December 1941.

The events of war brought about an unexpected alliance between communist Russia and the capitalist West. The USA and Britain had pledged their support for democracy in the **Atlantic Charter** signed in 1941. The Soviet Union, however, was ruled by a one-party dictatorship.

The second front

The German invasion of 1941 took the USSR by surprise, and it quickly suffered millions of casualties. Only a determined effort stopped the Germans from taking Moscow and Leningrad (St Petersburg). In 1942 it then faced a further threat, as the Germans attacked Stalingrad. Losses were very high and, not surprisingly, Stalin looked to a British and US invasion of northern France for relief. German defences were not yet strong in northern France and the war in Russia took huge numbers of German resources. Invading and creating a second front would threaten Hitler with war on two fronts and relieve the terrible pressure on the USSR. Yet, despite Russian pleas, and indeed the support of leading US commanders, no second front was created until June 1944. British leaders were convinced that it would be too risky, especially after the failure of a raid on the occupied French port of Dieppe in 1942 incurred heavy casualties. Instead, British and US efforts were concentrated first on North Africa, then on an invasion of Sicily and Italy in 1943. Relatively limited land forces were involved, and casualties did not match the heavy losses suffered by the USSR. The suspicion in the USSR was that the capitalist West wanted the dictatorships to fight each other to a standstill.

The Russian advance, 1943–45

After the German failure at Stalingrad in February 1943, the Russians were able to go on the offensive. This opened up the possibility of Russian expansion in Eastern Europe. Stalin's decision not to support a Polish uprising in Warsaw in 1944 allowed the Germans to destroy resistance before Russia moved in to take the city, which alarmed the West. It seemed that Stalin was happy to see German forces destroy Polish patriots because this would make future Soviet control of Poland easier. This followed revelations of a Soviet massacre of influential Polish officers and leaders in Katyn Forest in 1940.

Military cooperation

Britain and the USA had collaborated closely in the war and the high point was D-Day, the joint invasion of France in June 1944. Though supplies and aid had gone to Russia, there were no similar joint military operations. Britain and the USA did not share the key military secret of the war – the development of atomic weapons – with the USSR. For its part, the USSR did not until the very end of the war join in the struggle against Japan.

Relations between the members of the alliance remained strained:
● The USA disliked the idea of a war that strengthened the British Empire, which it distrusted.
● Churchill feared Russian expansion and thought that the USA was not taking the threat seriously.
● Stalin thought that the West did not understand the sheer scale of Russian losses or that it was Russian forces that had borne the brunt of the war effort.

The wartime alliance gave way to **Cold War**.

! Delete as applicable

Below is a sample exam question and a paragraph written in answer to this question. Read the paragraph and decide which of the possible options (in bold) is the most appropriate.

'The Western powers provided the Soviet Union with little support during World War II.' How far do you agree?

It is **fair/unfair** to argue that the Western powers provided the Soviet Union with little support during World War II. The Western powers were **very quick/fairly quick/very slow** to provide assistance to the Soviet Union by opening up a second front to ease the pressure on Soviet forces. Churchill **promised to help/declined to give support to** Russia. Moreover, military aid **was/was not** sent to the Soviet Union from Britain, which was **very helpful/not very helpful** in enabling Russia to resist the German advance. However, there was **a great deal of/some/little** military cooperation with the Soviet Union and this was seen most clearly over the atom bomb. The West was **very concerned/somewhat concerned/pleased** by Soviet expansion and its advance westwards. The lack of support given by Russia to the Warsaw Uprising and the earlier discovery of the Katyn massacre **pleased/concerned** the Western powers as it would make Soviet control of Poland **harder/easier**. The Soviet Union believed that the West wanted it to **be victorious/be exhausted/expand** as a result of the conflict with Germany and that this would **strengthen/weaken** its position after the war. This made relations between the West and East **stronger/weaker**.

⦿ Support your judgement   **a**

Read the sample exam question and two basic judgements below. Support the judgement that you agree with most strongly by adding a reason that justifies this judgement.

Tip: whichever option you choose, you will have to weigh up both sides of the argument. You could use phrases and words such as 'whereas' or 'although' in order to help the process of evaluation.

'The wartime alliance between the West and East was a success.'

The wartime alliance was a success because...	The wartime alliance was a failure because...
_____	_____
_____	_____
_____	_____
_____	_____
_____	_____

Tensions and difficulties at the conference at Tehran

REVISED

Churchill, Stalin and **Roosevelt** met together for the first time at Tehran, from 28 November to 1 December 1943. By this time, the tide had turned after British victories in the Mediterranean and Russian advances following the German defeat at Stalingrad. The meeting of the **'big three'** considered key elements in a post-war world.

It confirmed the meeting of foreign ministers held in Moscow in October that had established a European Advisory Commission to discuss the partition of Germany and also issued a Declaration of General Security proposing a United Nations.

The United Nations

Roosevelt and Stalin discussed how the new UN would work, with the key roles of the 'four policemen' – Britain, the USA, the USSR and China – ensuring peace. This gave the USSR an importance in the new organisation that it had never had in the old League of Nations.

Poland and the Baltic

It was agreed that post-war Poland would be redrawn so that the boundary would be the Oder-Neisse Rivers. This involved moving the boundaries westwards, giving Russia the territories in eastern Poland that it had occupied in 1939–40. This was a sign that Russia would keep the lands it had taken and that the older boundaries of pre-1917 Russia would be restored. Russia would also keep the Baltic states of Latvia, Lithuania and Estonia, made independent after World War I. This was hugely significant as Britain had gone to war in 1939 in defence of Poland but now was accepting a major change in its boundaries.

Japan

Roosevelt secured Stalin's agreement to declare war on Japan at a future date in return for territories – South Sakhalin, the Kurile Islands and access to Port Arthur.

The invasion of France

The invasion of northern France by Britain and the USA was agreed for May 1944. Churchill would have preferred an invasion of the Balkans but the pressure was now irresistible. Stalin agreed to mount a major attack at the same time to distract German forces. This met the demand from Stalin for a second front.

Turkey

It was agreed that the Allies would persuade Turkey to enter the war in return for support. This did not occur until 1945.

Germany

The conference discussed the future partition of Germany, which would be raised in the Moscow Conference (December 1945).

Winners and losers

- Roosevelt had gained Russian support – at least in the future – against Japan and had taken Britain away from a Balkan invasion to the policy favoured by the USA, of an invasion of northern France. He had established good personal relations with Stalin.
- Stalin's military victories in 1943 gave him prestige. The other world leaders had travelled a long way to meet him, while he was relatively close to home and the conference took place in the Soviet Embassy. He had gained the Allies' acceptance of expansion into Eastern Europe and an agreement for a second front in northern Europe. The USSR was set to play a much greater part in international affairs in the future United Nations. He had also divided Roosevelt and Churchill. Their personal relations at Tehran were much less close than they had been.
- Churchill, on the other hand, felt slighted by private meetings during the conference between Roosevelt and Stalin and by Roosevelt's coolness towards him. Britain was committed to a second front despite Churchill's grave misgivings. Large areas of Poland were to be given to Russia, which was a blow to Britain's prestige as it had gone to war in 1939 specifically to defend Polish independence against Germany.

The Tehran Conference was a major turning point in the re-emergence of Russia as a major world power and key decisions were taken or confirmed about the post-war world.

Develop the detail

Below is a sample exam question and a paragraph written in answer to this question. The paragraph contains a limited amount of detail. Annotate it to add additional detail to the answer.

'Churchill failed in his aims at the Tehran Conference.' How far do you agree?

> Churchill had a number of aims at Tehran. He had some limited success, but there were more failures, most notably over the second front and his failure to secure agreement on his preferred policy. Churchill was concerned about the increasing presence of the Soviets in the East of Europe, particularly given the reason why Britain had gone to war. Churchill was also concerned about his relationship with Roosevelt and the improvement in relations between Roosevelt and Stalin.

Introducing an argument

Below is a sample exam question, a list of key points to be made in the answer, and a simple introduction and conclusion for the answer. Read these and then, using the information on the opposite page, rewrite the introduction and the conclusion in order to develop an argument.

'The greatest success for the Soviet Union at the Tehran Conference was the territorial gain in Poland and the Baltic.' How far do you agree?

Key points

- Russia gained the territories in eastern Poland, which it had occupied in 1939–40.
- Russia would keep the Baltic states.
- The Western powers agreed to open a second front in May 1944.
- Stalin had gained acceptance of Soviet expansion in Eastern Europe.
- The USSR was set to play a greater role in world affairs.
- Stalin had been able to divide Roosevelt and Churchill.

Introduction

> There were many successes for the Soviet Union at the Tehran Conference. Stalin had been able to make territorial gains in both Poland and the Baltic states. He had been able to gain acceptance for further Soviet expansion in Eastern Europe. Stalin was also pleased as he was able to secure agreement from the Western powers to open a second front in France, something Churchill had been reluctant to do. With the Soviet victories against Germany, it had increased its prestige and would play a greater role in world affairs. Its position was further enhanced by the division Stalin had created between Roosevelt and Churchill.

Conclusion

> To conclude, there were many reasons why the Tehran Conference was a success for the Soviets. Not only had they made territorial gains, taking back land in the Baltic and Poland, but they had secured agreement for further advances. Their success was further enhanced as they were now seen as a major power and their position was further strengthened by the divisions they had encouraged between Roosevelt and Churchill, which also made the conference a success for the Soviets.

Tensions and difficulties at the conferences at Yalta and Potsdam

Yalta, 4–11 February 1945

By the time the Yalta Conference took place in February 1945, there were more tensions between East and West. Churchill was concerned about the growing power of the USSR, as its forces controlled Eastern Europe. Stalin wanted the West to accept that Russian future security needed a broad zone of Eastern Europe that the USSR could control as a barrier against invasion.

Poland

Stalin saw the pro-Soviet Lublin Committee as the true representatives of Poland. Churchill feared that these Stalinists would exclude the democratic Polish representatives in London. It was agreed to enlarge the Lublin government and to hold free elections. There was little to guarantee, however, that Stalin would actually allow this.

Germany

Stalin wanted to take German machinery, food and goods. Churchill and the USA disagreed, doubting the wisdom of having millions of poor and starving people at the heart of Europe.

Germany would be divided into four zones of occupation. Churchill had insisted that France have a zone, fearful that the USA would withdraw after the war and leave Britain alone to face the USSR. Stalin initially refused to give France a say in running occupied Germany, but did finally agree.

The United Nations

Stalin wanted greater representation by the individual republics of the USSR, fearful that the United Nations would become anti-Soviet. Roosevelt saw the UN as the hope for the future, but Stalin feared it might become anti-communist.

Japan

Stalin agreed to declare war on Japan but demanded more than at Tehran, with railway rights in Chinese Manchuria and access to the Chinese port of Darien. Roosevelt was forced to agree.

Potsdam, 17 July to 2 August 1945

With 10 million Soviet troops deployed in Europe, there was little to be done if Stalin imposed his will on Eastern Europe. Yalta had shown weaknesses on the part of Britain and the USA in meeting Russian demands and this resulted in a more difficult summit at Potsdam.

Problems at Potsdam

- The new president **Harry S Truman** was more suspicious of Stalin and the USSR's ambitions.
- Churchill had been voted out of office in the middle of the conference. The less emotional Labour prime minister Attlee lacked Churchill's rapport with Stalin, and Ernest Bevin, the foreign secretary, was hostile to communism.
- Aid to the USSR under the **Lend-Lease scheme** was cut off by the USA on 8 May and restored until September only after Russian protests.
- It was clear that Stalin did not intend to share power in Poland. The arrest of 16 non-communists who had gone back to Warsaw in the hope of taking part in a free election campaign was worrying.
- There was also the issue of the atomic bomb, which Truman mentioned to Stalin, though the Russians were already aware of the development of the new weapon.

There was agreement but many issues were unresolved and the Potsdam Conference did not result in any general peace settlement.

Germany

There would be an Allied Control Commission made up of the military commanders of the four zones of occupation. The Soviets, however, insisted on complete control of their own zone. There was little overall government for Germany.

Reparations were agreed on, but the policies were very different in each zone. An agreement that 15 per cent of reparations from the West would go to the Russian zone in return for food and raw materials did not work.

Eastern Europe

There was no firm agreement on the western frontier and this was left for a future peace conference. The Western powers supported elections in Soviet-held territory in Poland, Hungary, Romania and Bulgaria, but there was no means of enforcing this.

Spectrum of importance

Below is a sample exam question and a list of general points that could be used to answer the question. Use your own knowledge, and the information on the opposite page and from earlier in the book, to reach a judgement about the seriousness of the divisions faced by the Allies at the Yalta and Potsdam Conferences. Write numbers on the spectrum below to indicate their relative seriousness. Having done this, write a brief justification of your placement, explaining why some of the divisions were more serious than others. The resulting diagram could form the basis of an essay plan.

How serious were the divisions between the Allies at the Yalta and Potsdam Conferences?

1 Stalin wanted a buffer zone in Eastern Europe against future invasion. 2 ·

2 Disagreements over the nature of the Polish government. 5 ·

3 Stalin wanted to take German machinery and goods as compensation. 4 ·

4 Stalin did not want France to have a role in the running of Germany. 8 ·

5 Attitudes towards the United Nations and the representation of republics of the USSR. 1 ·

6 Agreement over reparations from the Western zones of Germany failed. 7 ·

7 There was failure to agree a western frontier in Eastern Europe. 3 ·

8 The USA temporarily suspended Lend-Lease to the USSR. 6 ·

Least serious ⟵⟶ Most serious

 Challenge the historian   **a**

Below is a sample AS exam question including an interpretation written by a historian. You must read the extract, identify the argument in the interpretation, and use your own knowledge to support and provide a counter-argument, challenging the interpretation offered.

'It seems clear that some form of tension between the USA and USSR would have sprung up following the end of World War II. The two new superpowers were competing for influence in a new international order.'

Source: D. Murphy, The Cold War 1945–49

Evaluate the strengths and limitations of this interpretation, making reference to other interpretations you have studied.

1 What is the view of the interpretation?

_____

_____

2 What knowledge of your own do you have that supports the interpretation?

_____

_____

3 What knowledge of your own do you have that challenges the interpretation?

_____

_____

The 'liberation of Europe in the East and West'

The suffering of the USSR had been considerably greater during the war than that of the USA and Britain. When the Red Army moved into Eastern Europe, it was to impose Russian domination and to take revenge on its enemies. This was partly a result of the brutalisation brought by the regime and partly in pursuit of restoring traditional Russian spheres of influence and ensuring future Russian security. The difference in ideologies between East and West also made it seem that the expansion was motivated by a desire to export Marxist–Leninism.

Western liberation

The first area to be liberated was Italy. The removal of Mussolini in 1943 helped the Allies to see Italy as an ally rather than as an enemy, and Italian opponents of fascism assisted the Allied advance. The Allied forces in France, the Low Countries and Denmark were seen as liberators. They brought much-needed supplies to areas short of food. There was clearly no thought of annexing territory or imposing an ideology in these areas.

The situation was more complex in Greece, where Britain supported the royalists in a civil war from 1944 to prevent a communist state.

The invasion of Germany by Western forces saw hard-fought conflict but not a war of revenge or reprisal. Once fighting stopped, aid was given to German civilians.

Eastern liberation

Revenge

The experience in Eastern Europe was very different. The larger Soviet forces inflicted a much harsher retribution on Germany and its allies. There were terrible reprisals against civilians and the Soviet army was guilty of indiscriminate sexual assaults on females. There was much plunder and removal of goods and machinery. There was also deportation of prisoners for work in the USSR and the forced removal of ethnic Germans from annexed territories.

Annexation

In terms of asserting power, the pre-1918 Russian territories were restored to Russian control and opposition suppressed. The Baltic states and eastern Poland, taken illegally in 1939–40, returned to Russian control. The presence of the Red Army in Eastern Europe had quite different significance to that of the presence of the armies of Britain and the USA in the West. It led to direct annexation of territory in Poland, Finland, the Baltic states, Germany, Czechoslovakia and Romania. Russia regained an area of 470,000 square km and 24 million people. This had no parallel in the West.

Political influence

As well as direct annexation, there was the spread of Russian political domination in nations that were nominally independent but in practice were dominated by the USSR. This was on a large scale – over 1 million square km and 90 million people.

The Russian forces were deeply involved with politics:
- They supported a coup in Romania in 1945, forcing the king to appoint a communist government.
- They installed a coalition in Hungary, which included communists who would later take over the state.
- Soviet forces controlled Bulgaria in a special Allied Control Council set up in 1944.
- In Poland, Soviet forces established a National Liberation Committee, which had communist influence out of all proportion to the support the communist parties enjoyed in Poland.
- In Czechoslovakia, negotiations between the communists and other groups were strengthened by the Soviet military presence.
- In Germany, the Soviet forces created a new left-wing party, the SED. This degree of political influence had no parallel in the West.

There was widespread political repression and control; 47,000 anti-communist Poles were arrested in 1944–45. There was also much less direct aid given to the peoples of Eastern Europe than was the case in the West.

! Concept map

Make a copy of the concept map below and use the information on the opposite page and page 18 to add detail to it, showing how important the social and economic differences were.

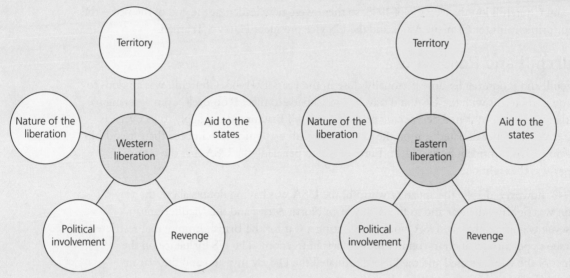

♦ Support your judgement   a

Read the sample exam question and two basic judgements below. Support the judgement that you agree with most strongly by adding a reason that justifies this judgement.

Tip: whichever option you choose, you will have to weigh up both sides of the argument. You could use phrases and words such as 'whereas' or 'although' in order to help the process of evaluation.

'The most serious consequence of the liberation of Eastern Europe was the political domination of the USSR.' How far do you agree?

Overall, the most serious consequence of the liberation of Eastern Europe was the political domination of the USSR...

_____

_____

_____

_____

_____

However, it was not the political domination of the USSR but the annexation of territory that was the most important consequence of the liberation of Eastern Europe...

_____

_____

_____

_____

_____

Relations between Stalin, Churchill and Roosevelt (and later Truman and Attlee)

The so-called big three leaders had been Churchill, Roosevelt and Stalin. Roosevelt died in April 1945 and Churchill lost the election of 1945, so there were new leaders at the end of the war – the Labour prime minister Clement Attlee and the US vice president Harry S Truman.

Churchill and Roosevelt

Churchill and Roosevelt became personally close in the years 1941–43. Churchill was anxious to keep on good terms with the USA and travelled to Canada to meet Roosevelt, even agreeing to an Atlantic Charter of shared democratic principles, which Britain did not apply to its overseas empire. When Hitler declared war on the USA, Churchill was quick to reinforce their friendship and gain US commitment to the war in Europe, and to persuade the USA that the British strategy was the right one.

By 1943, however, despite the apparent warmth, the USA was having doubts about the way Britain was fighting the war and its focus on war in North Africa and the Mediterranean. Roosevelt was afraid that the USA would be fighting a war for the British Empire that restricted US trade opportunities and ran counter to its beliefs in freedom. The US influence on the conduct of the war increased and the USA dominated the D-Day invasion and the war in northern France and Germany 1944–45.

Churchill and Stalin

Churchill was also anxious to establish good relations with the USSR once the Germans invaded Russia in 1941. In his dealings with Stalin there was a remarkable amount of mutual respect and even goodwill. Years of past hostility to communism and underlying fears that Russia would dominate Europe made the relationship strained, however. Churchill was unwilling to agree to Stalin's demands for a second front (see page 10) and was increasingly alarmed about the advance of Russian forces after 1943. Britain had gone to war to defend Poland and yet by 1944 was having to accept its domination by the USSR. In October 1944 Churchill went to Moscow to try and broker a deal and secured the so-called Percentages Agreement, that Eastern Europe would be divided between Russia and the West into spheres of influence. This showed the contempt both leaders had for the wishes of the people of Eastern Europe. This was never put into practice, as the USA would not have agreed.

Roosevelt and Stalin

Roosevelt was less concerned with the possible domination of Eastern Europe. He believed that he could get deals with Stalin over elections in Russian-occupied territories and needed Russia to enter the war against Japan, which was taking an increasingly heavy toll on US forces.

By 1945 Roosevelt had accepted Russian domination of Eastern Europe; the division of Germany was agreed, as was a new United Nations organisation for peace, but with safeguards against any possible condemnation of Russian actions. Churchill had realised that Britain could no longer exert the major influence on world affairs.

New leaders

The changes in leadership after Yalta brought new leaders. Attlee and Truman had little experience of foreign affairs, and the strong personal relations between the 'big three' could no longer guide international affairs. Truman had less inclination to make concessions to Stalin, and Attlee's foreign minister, Bevin, was a tough negotiator who disliked communism. The realities of Russian influence in the East (see above) were hitting home and at the Potsdam Conference it was harder to bring about decisive solutions. No general peace settlement ended the war, and Truman and Stalin were poised for the confrontations of the Cold War.

Simple essay style

Below is a sample exam question. Use your own knowledge, and the information on the opposite page and in other sections of the book, to produce a plan for this question. Choose four general points, and provide three pieces of specific information to support each general point. Once you have planned your essay, write the introduction and conclusion for it. The introduction should list the points to be discussed in the essay and outline the line of argument you intend to take. The conclusion should summarise the main points and justify which point was the most important.

> 'Roosevelt was more successful than Churchill in his dealings with Stalin.' How far do you agree?

 Develop the detail   **a**

Below is a sample exam question and a paragraph written in answer to this question. The paragraph contains a limited amount of detail. Annotate it to add additional detail to the answer.

> 'Churchill's relationship with Roosevelt was a great success.' How far do you agree?

The two leaders were very close in the early years of the war. Churchill travelled to meet Roosevelt and signed an agreement with him, even though it was a threat to the British Empire. Churchill was able to gain Roosevelt's support for the war and initially for his strategy. However, the relationship changed because of the direction of British attacks. Roosevelt believed that this did not benefit US needs or beliefs. Eventually, Roosevelt was able to force his views on Churchill.

Exam focus

Below is a sample exam-style question and a model answer. Read them and the comments around the answer.

Assess the reasons for the growth of tensions between the USSR and the West between 1946 and 1949.

Tensions between the USSR and the West developed in the period between 1946 and 1949 for a number of reasons, however it must be remembered that difficulties already existed due to ideological differences and disagreements during World War II. These had already become very apparent once the threat of the common enemy, in the form of Nazi Germany, had been defeated. It would therefore be fair to argue that the tensions of 1946–49 built on pre-existing suspicions and were simply made worse by each side's fears of the other, particularly over nuclear weapons and events in Eastern Europe.

A clear view is offered, but the events are also placed in the wider context of tensions.

Tensions between the USSR and the West were not new and can be traced back to the 1917 Bolshevik takeover, which had led to the establishment of anti-capitalist ideology and challenged Western values. With the USSR seeking to spread its ideology and the West concerned by this threat, it is hardly surprising that tensions existed even before 1946. The World War II alliance against Nazi Germany only papered over these tensions and, even then, tensions still existed. The USSR believed that the delay by the Western powers in launching the second front was a deliberate attempt to weaken it and ensure that it faced the full force of the Nazi military machine. On the other hand, the West was concerned about Soviet plans for Eastern Europe once 'liberation' had begun, particularly in Greece, and distrust was simply reinforced by events such as the Katyn massacre and the Soviet attitude towards the Warsaw Uprising.

The view in the opening paragraph is explained and developed. It is well supported by precise examples from both sides of the Cold War.

These tensions were only further developed by events at the end of the war. The USA failed to share its development of the atomic bomb with the USSR and this monopoly of atomic weapons by the West was a particular concern in the USSR. It increased its sense of vulnerability, while it was also bitter that the development of the weapon had been kept secret. On the other hand, the West was concerned about the presence of the large Red Army in Eastern Europe and the threat this posed to Western security, as it was far larger than Western forces. Therefore, as the war ended, both sides were suspicious of the intentions of the other and it was already apparent that the wartime alliance was under strain and that the only thing uniting the two sides was a common enemy. These pre-existing tensions meant it was almost inevitable that both sides would view the actions of the other with suspicion, which simply encouraged a further escalation in tensions. Events both before and during World War II meant that there was already distrust, and the aims and ambitions of both sides only added to this.

The point is developed further, again with reference to specific events, to show how deep-seated the mistrust was even during and immediately after the war.

The USA's policy of containment, with the Truman Plan, was viewed by the USSR as aggressive and its offer of economic aid was viewed as 'dollar diplomacy' and an attempt to weaken the Soviet Union's influence in Eastern Europe. The Marshall Plan was a particular challenge to the Soviet Union and forced it to consolidate its hold on Eastern Europe, which worried politicians in the West. The Soviets saw US actions as provocative, as the

Marshall Plan aimed not just to stop the spread of communism, but in the long term to pull the Eastern European states out of the Soviet orbit. This therefore threatened Soviet security. On the other hand, the West viewed the actions of the Soviet Union as a threat, going against the agreements made earlier about free elections. The West was concerned about Soviet intentions and the extent of the spread of communism, particularly given the economic conditions in much of Western Europe and the strength of the communist parties in some states, such as Italy and France. The Soviet Union, however, viewed its actions in countries such as Czechoslovakia, where a coup brought the communists to power, as essential for its own security through a buffer zone. The West viewed this as further evidence of Soviet power spreading further west. It was the very different interpretations of the actions of each side by the other side that did much to increase the already existing tensions.

Tensions developed most noticeably over Germany and its future. Its geographical position made it crucial in Europe, and its division, and that of Berlin, between the four powers at the end of the war provided the opportunity for further crises. Once again, the actions of both powers simply increased tensions. The Soviets viewed Germany as a source of reparations to make up for their wartime losses and were fearful that the West wanted to rebuild Germany, not just as a market for its goods but as an anti-Soviet ally. These fears appeared to be confirmed by the currency reforms that were introduced in the Western zones. It was this development that ultimately led to the greatest sign of increased tensions: the Berlin blockade. This showed how deep Soviet concerns were about control of Germany, but also that the West was willing to risk confrontation with the USSR to prevent Soviet expansion westwards.

Although many events increased tensions between the two sets of powers, it was the long-term causes of the tension, particularly the difference in ideology and the fear from the West of the spread of communism and the belief of the Soviet Union that the West wanted to destroy it, that provided the basis for all the tensions. The developments that took place in the post-war years all developed out of the mistrust that had already existed and had only been put on hold to defeat a common enemy in World War II.

The argument is balanced, considering how the Soviet view of key developments in US policy increased tensions and similarly how Soviet actions worried the West.

A further cause of tensions is examined and an explanation as to how and why it increased tensions is offered.

The conclusion picks up on the view offered in the opening paragraph and develops it to explain why long-term tensions were the most important factor. There has been consistency of argument throughout the response.

The answer is well focused on the demands of the question and supports the argument with precise and relevant examples. There is a clear line of argument throughout the essay and the view offered in the opening paragraph is developed throughout the main body of the answer. There is much more that could have been considered, for example the development of the satellite states, but in the time allowed examiners will not expect everything to be covered. The answer is balanced and there is clear judgement, which will take it to the top level.

Reaching a judgement

In order to reach the very top level, you need to reach judgements about the issue you are considering in relation to the question. Identify the paragraphs where this candidate has successfully done this, and those where a judgement is either absent or not well developed. In the latter case, write a couple of sentences for each paragraph so that a judgement is reached based on the argument.

Exam focus

Below is a sample short-answer question and a model answer. Read them and the comments around the answer.

Which of the following did more to increase tensions between the West and the USSR in the period to the end of 1945?

(i)   The delays over the opening of a second front.

(ii)   The liberation of Eastern Europe.

There were tensions within the wartime alliance throughout the war, made stronger by the ideological differences and the Soviet Union's former alliance with Nazi Germany. Throughout the war, both sides remained suspicious of the motives of the other and this was seen in their views of the delays in opening a second front and the liberation of Eastern Europe. It was the liberation of Eastern Europe, however, that was the most important factor in creating tensions, as it led to the permanent division of Europe.

The delays over the opening of a second front did create tensions, as Stalin believed that the decision not to invade France until June 1944 was a plot to ensure the overthrow of communism by Nazi Germany. He believed that the West wanted Germany and Russia to bleed each other dry so that the West would easily be able to take over. He failed to understand that the West did not believe that an amphibious landing would be successful, particularly after the Dieppe fiasco, as the Atlantic Wall was not complete. The West appeared not to appreciate the pressures that Soviet forces were under in the East. Stalin wanted the West to help relieve the pressure by forcing Germany to divert some of its forces. It led him to consider a possible secret peace with Germany up to September 1943, while the West, aware of such considerations, viewed Stalin as untrustworthy. It was this that led the Soviet Communist foreign minister Andrei Gromyko to argue that the Cold War began as a 'secret Cold War when the Allies delayed the opening of the second front in Europe.'

The liberation of Europe was more significant in the development of tensions, as the West did not simply see Stalin's actions as an attempt to protect the USSR from any future German attack, but as a pretext for expansion and even to create global communism. Tensions were created as, at least in part, the West failed to understand the scale of the sacrifices the Soviet Union had made, with some 25 million dead, and the damage that had been done to its economy and therefore its need for reparations. Although agreements were reached between the Allies at Yalta and Potsdam, these did little to lessen tensions as the USSR failed to keep some of the promises made and free elections were not held in Poland or Romania. Stalin's desire for pro-Soviet regimes in areas such as Hungary and Czechoslovakia and the presence of Soviet troops in Germany increased tensions as the West was worried by the presence of such a large force and the fear that Soviet power would spread even further west.

A clear view is offered, but the events are also placed in the wider context of tensions.

The importance of delays in opening the second front are explained and its significance in causing tensions explored. The quotation from Gromyko is particularly useful in showing a Soviet view of its importance.

The second issue is explained and the significance considered. There is some precise factual material to support the argument.

Although the constant delays in opening the second front did cause tensions, the supply of weapons to the USSR helped to ease some of the concerns, as did Roosevelt's diplomacy and pressure on Churchill. Moreover, the tensions were eased by the events of D-Day. The tensions caused by the Soviet liberation of Eastern Europe were not resolved, however, and got only worse. The attitudes of the two powers to the liberation and the concepts of freedom and democracy served to show the gulf between the two sides and led to long-term hostility. The common enemy meant the delays over the second front did not prevent cooperation during the war, but the liberation of Eastern Europe appeared to betray the very reasons for the war against Nazi Germany and therefore had a greater impact on relations between the East and the West.

A very strong judgement is reached. There is a good comparison between the two issues and a supported conclusion is reached.

The answer is well focused on the two issues and examines the importance of both in the developing tensions. The factors are analysed and there is relevant and accurate knowledge present to support the argument. The two factors are compared and there is a supported judgement as to why the liberation of Eastern Europe was more important.

Reaching a judgement

In order to reach the higher levels, you must reach a judgement as to which factor was the more important. This response argues that it was the liberation of Eastern Europe. Use the information in the answer to rewrite the conclusion to argue that the delays in launching the second front were more important.

Exam focus (AS-level)

Below is a sample AS-level interpretation question and a model answer. Read them and the comments around the answer.

'The Cold War was not inevitable; yet it became a reality because of the innate needs of the Soviet Union and the United States.'

Source: M. McCauley The Origins of the Cold War

Evaluate the strengths and limitations of this interpretation, making reference to other interpretations that you have studied.

The interpretation puts forward the view that the Cold War was not inevitable, but that it came about because of the needs of the USSR and the USA. There has been much debate about why the Cold War broke out, with some arguing that it was likely given the tensions between the USA and the USSR since the 1917 Revolution and their views on capitalism and socialism, which were compounded by disagreements during the war. Other interpretations have stressed that the outbreak was due more to one country than the other, with some putting forward the view that the USSR was to blame and others the USA. Some interpretations have suggested that both were to blame.

The interpretation is partially correct in suggesting that the needs of the two countries were crucial in the outbreak as there was fear in the United States that the Soviet Union wanted to spread communism, while in the Soviet Union there was concern that it was isolated and needed to create a series of buffer states in Eastern Europe in order to preserve its very existence. The interpretation is also valid as both sides had contributed significantly to the defeat of Nazism and the Axis powers; the Soviet Union in particular had lost large numbers and seen its economy severely damaged, and therefore needed to gain reparations from Germany. This served only to further increase tensions. These problems were only added to by the death of Roosevelt and his replacement by Truman, who was more fearful about the spread of communism. Similarly, the interpretation is correct in that the Cold War was not inevitable as the two sides had worked together to defeat Nazism and the USA had supported the USSR in the argument to open a second front. Moreover, Roosevelt had developed a close working relationship with Stalin, as seen at Yalta, and this suggests the Cold War was far from inevitable.

The view in the interpretation is explained and is placed in the wider context of the debate about the origins of the Cold War. No reference is made to historiography, but this is not a requirement of this paper.

The strength of the interpretation is explained. Own knowledge is clearly linked to the interpretation and is precise and well chosen to support the points made. The response uses a range of evaluative words.

There are, however, limitations to the interpretation as it ignores the policies adopted by both the USSR and the USA. It fails to recognise that the policies and attitude of the USA could be seen to provoke the USSR, with Kennan's Long Telegram in February 1946 and the Truman Doctrine or the economic policies it adopted, particularly the Marshall Plan. It could also be argued that the interpretation is limited as it does not consider the role of the USSR in bringing about the Cold War by its refusal to cooperate over European issues and the establishment of satellite states in Eastern Europe through salami tactics. The interpretation also argues that the Cold War was not inevitable, and yet the hostility from capitalism towards the Soviet Union following its adoption of Marxism–Leninism made it more likely, and that the two nations were brought together in the early 1940s only because of a shared hostility towards Nazism and the threat it posed to them both.

Therefore, although there are some strengths to the view, there are also some limitations and it would probably be fair to argue that it offers only a partial view of the origins of the Cold War. While it may be correct to argue that nothing is inevitable, there were sufficient long-term disagreements to suggest the relationship was unlikely to be easy.

Similarly in this paragraph, there is clear evaluation of the limitations. There is much that could be said, but it is not expected that all possible issues will be discussed. There is sufficient evidence here to show that the learner is aware of the limitations.

Although a judgement is not required, the learner does pull the material together and suggests that they, in part at least, disagree with the view offered.

The answer explains the interpretation and places it in the wider context of the historical debate about the issue and whether the Cold War broke out because of the innate needs of the two powers. Detailed knowledge is directly applied to the interpretation to show both its strengths and its limitations, and throughout the response the focus remains on evaluating the given interpretation, not other interpretations.

Reverse engineering

Answers to interpretation questions should start by placing the given interpretation in the wider context of the historical debate about the issue. This interpretation is about the Cold War not being inevitable, but being due to the needs of the two superpowers. Rewrite the response in answer to an interpretation that argues the Cold War was inevitable.

The importance of Churchill's Iron Curtain speech

In opposition, **Churchill** was freer to give his views on the international situation. He was increasingly concerned that:

- Britain and the USA had allowed the **USSR** to dominate Eastern Europe
- the USA might withdraw from Europe and retreat into isolation, not understanding what he saw as the threat from communism.

In March 1946 Churchill made a speech, which he called 'The Sinews of Peace', in Fulton, Missouri. The speech was not all hostile to **Stalin**, but it used a phrase that became famous:

> From Stettin in the Baltic to Trieste in the Adriatic, an *iron curtain* has descended across the continent.

He referred to the great capitals of Eastern Europe – 'Warsaw, Berlin, Prague, Vienna, Budapest, Belgrade, Bucharest and Sofia' – being behind that curtain in the Soviet sphere. He referred to the 'indefinite expansion of its power and doctrines'. He saw Stalin as admiring strength and despising weakness and urged a settlement with him 'supported by the whole strength of the English-speaking world'.

Key ideas

The following ideas were central to Churchill's speech:
- Europe was firmly divided.
- The USSR controlled all the Eastern European countries equally.
- The West needed to negotiate from a position of strength.
- The USSR wanted to expand without limit.
- The USSR wanted to expand not only its power but the doctrine of communism.

Goebbels, the Nazi propaganda minister, had used the key phrase 'iron curtain'. That did not stop it becoming highly influential, and the term 'the Iron Curtain Countries' became widespread to describe the '**Soviet bloc**', or Eastern Europe in general. It summed up a lot of developing fears in the USA that Russia was expansionist and intent on imposing control, and has been seen as a spur to US policies of opposition to the spread of communism (see page 30).

Reactions to the speech

- Stalin reacted by arguing that the USSR, having lost so many people in the war, had a right to take measures to ensure its security and had only peaceful ambitions to ensure that neighbouring states were loyal. He accused Churchill of being 'a firebrand of war'.
- Many in the USA thought the speech was irresponsible and one newspaper described it as 'poisonous'. **Truman** did not immediately signify his approval.
- Though the phrase 'iron curtain' was influential, the speech did not in itself change US policy, which was moving towards the idea of opposing any expansion of communism. Churchill's speech was much less important than the views of influential foreign policy experts like George F. Kennan, who warned of traditional Russian ambitions and desire for expansion and of the need to oppose these.
- By 1946 the mood in the USA was shifting away from possible isolationism to meeting the dangers of communist expansion. The speech did more to confirm changing views than to create them.

Accuracy and importance

The content of the speech was flawed. The rigid demarcation of West and East did not amount to an iron curtain in 1946 and Soviet influence was not as uniform as Churchill made out. Berlin was not under total Soviet control, nor was Vienna. In Belgrade, the capital of Yugoslavia, it was not as strong as in other capitals. Total Soviet domination was not yet established in Prague. The speech showed little awareness of Soviet security needs and concerns and made assumptions about 'indefinite expansionism' and respect for sheer force. Stalin, for example, had not attempted to intervene in Greece. The vivid image of the speech, however, helped to encourage anti-Russian sentiment – and provoked equally strong rhetoric from the USSR, ramping up tension and verbal conflict.

Support or challenge? a

Below is a sample exam question that asks how far you agree with a specific statement. Below this is a series of general statements that are relevant to the question. Using your own knowledge and the information on the opposite page, decide whether each statement supports or challenges the statement in the question and tick the appropriate box.

'Churchill's Iron Curtain speech had little impact.' How far do you agree?

	Support	Challenge
The term 'iron curtain' became widely used to describe the Soviet bloc.		
Stalin argued that the Soviet Union had a right to ensure its own security after the losses of the war.		
US policy did not change after the speech.		
Many considered Churchill's speech to be irresponsible.		
The views of foreign policy experts, such as George Kennan, were more important.		
The speech did not change US views about the Soviet Union, but simply confirmed them.		
Truman did not immediately give his support to Churchill's views.		
Some of Churchill's claims, such as Berlin being under Russian control, were inaccurate.		
The speech encouraged anti-Russian sentiment.		

Recommended reading

Below is a list of suggested further reading on the origins and early development of the Cold War.
- D.G. Williamson, *The Cold War 1941–1995* (third edition, 2015)
- M. McCauley, *The Origins of the Cold War, 1941–49* (1995)
- D. Yergin, *Shattered Peace: The Origins of the Cold War and the National Security State* (1977)
- J.L. Gaddis, *The United States and the Origins of the Cold War, 1941–47* (2000)
- O. Edwards, *The USA and the Cold War* (1997)
- J. Smith, *The Cold War 1945–1965* (1989)

The impact of Soviet control of Eastern Europe on the Cold War

At Yalta in February 1945, **Roosevelt** had persuaded Stalin and Churchill to accept the Declaration on Liberated Europe. This emphasised the right of all peoples to choose the form of government under which to live.

By 1948 it was apparent that this had not been upheld in Eastern Europe. In lands annexed by the USSR, there was no choice for the inhabitants (see page 16).

Poland

Soviet forces had set up a new Provisional Government in June 1945 that was dominated by the Polish communists, who had little support in the country. It was obvious when the Polish government in exile in London joined that there would not be free elections. The non-communist Peasant Party representatives resigned in protest.

Romania

A new government was imposed on the king by the USSR in December 1945. Stalin created a new communist-dominated National Democratic Front in 1946. By violence and pressure, this won 80 per cent of the vote in the election of November 1946. In December 1947, the king was forced to abdicate and a Communist People's Republic was formed in April 1948.

The Soviet zone of Germany

The socialist SPD was forced to merge with the communists to form a Socialist Unity Party after large numbers of arrests of SPD members. This new party would be the basis of government when an independent East Germany was established in 1949.

Bulgaria

Stalin at first insisted that the communists who dominated the government accept non-communist members and that they accept the election results of October 1946, which gave a third of the votes to non-communist parties. By 1947, however, Stalin allowed the communists to repress all opposition, with the backing of the Russian army.

Hungary

In Hungary, Stalin did allow free elections in November 1945. In 1947 the leading opposition leader was arrested and increasing Soviet control was subsequently established. In March 1948, the socialists were forced to merge with the Hungarian communists and this new Independent Front was the only party.

Czechoslovakia

The elections of March 1946 gave the Czech communists 38 per cent of the vote, and were genuinely free. The Czech leader, Beneš, had been able to work with the Czech communists, but in 1947 there was more pressure for communist domination. The USSR was determined to prevent the Czechs from accepting US Marshall Aid (see page 30) and in February 1948 a communist coup with Soviet support took place.

Greece and Finland

Stalin did not intervene in the civil war in Greece, and also did not attempt to control Finland after a peace treaty in 1947 gave the naval base at Petsamo to the USSR.

Elements of Soviet domination

- The Russians and their allies had used **'salami tactics'**. That is, they had entered into pacts with other political parties, then when the time was right had 'sliced them' out of the coalition governments.
- The USSR had also used forced mergers with socialist parties to strengthen its position, as the socialists were dominated by communists backed by the Soviet army.
- Elections were carefully controlled by violence and intimidation.
- There was extensive propaganda and the establishment of political police.
- By 1948, unrepresentative pro-Moscow communist leaders had been established and opposition destroyed by arrests, intimidation and murder.

Western suspicion of Russian ambitions in Eastern Europe led to counter-measures in the form of the policy of **containment** in 1947. This in turn led to greater Russian control being imposed, so **Cold War** tensions escalated.

Simple essay style

Below is a sample exam question. Use your own knowledge, and the information on the opposite page and in other sections of the book, to produce a plan for this question. Choose four general points, and provide three pieces of specific information to support each general point. Once you have planned your essay, write the introduction and conclusion for it. The introduction should list the points to be discussed in the essay and outline the line of argument you intend to take. The conclusion should summarise the main points and justify which point was the most important.

'There was little popular support in the states of Eastern Europe for the establishment of communist regimes.' How far do you agree?

 Develop the detail　　　　　　　　　　　　　　　　　　　　　**a**

Below is a sample exam question and a paragraph written in answer to this question. The paragraph contains a limited amount of detail. Annotate it to add additional detail to the answer.

'The use of intimidation was the most important way the Soviet Union gained control in Eastern Europe.' How far do you agree?

> The Soviet Union used a range of methods and tactics to gain control in Eastern Europe. In many states non-communist parties were merged with the communists, who soon dominated the new party. This eventually led to the situation whereby the communists were the only party allowed to stand for election, or if opposition was allowed it faced intimidation. The Soviets also used the army in some countries to help impose their domination, while in other states the opposition was either arrested or, in some places, resigned in protest.

The Truman Doctrine and Marshall Aid

On 12 March 1947, Truman appealed for Congress to strengthen non-communist forces in areas thought to be vulnerable to possible communist domination.

- He set out his view of competing ways of life. The first had free institutions, **representative government**, free elections, guarantees of individual liberty, freedom of speech and religion, and freedom from oppression. The second was based on the will of a minority forcibly imposed on the majority, using terror and oppression.
- It was the policy of the USA to support free peoples who resist attempted 'subjugation by armed minorities or outside pressures'.
- It recognised that political extremism and dictatorship had its origins in misery and want; its seeds 'grow in the evil soil of poverty'.

The follow-up was the Marshall Plan of June 1947, in which the secretary for state George Marshall offered an aid package to Europe. No distinction was made between 'free' and 'unfree' countries. Stalin, however, forbade the Soviet-dominated nations to attend a meeting in Paris, attended by 16 nations. Congress approved the policy in 1948. An Organisation for European Economic Development was set up to promote common growth policies, but the aid was deployed by US representatives and the individual Western European governments with limited overall planning.

Why were these policies adopted?

- The USA could no longer rely on Britain, which had economic problems and overstretched forces, to guarantee that Greece and Turkey would remain free from communism.
- More fighting had broken out in Greece in September 1946 and Stalin had allowed communist forces from other Balkan countries to assist the Greek communists, contrary to his earlier policy.
- By 1947 it was clear that Stalin was not keeping to the agreement made at Yalta about elections in Eastern Europe.
- There were large communist parties in Italy and Germany, and communist forces were fighting against US-backed nationalists in China.

- The expansion of communism was not only against US ideology but also a threat to its economic interests.
- It was widely held that the rise of dictatorships and expansionist regimes between the wars had owed much to poverty and depression. It was, therefore, in the interests of the USA to use its wealth to prevent this recurring and being drawn in again to a European war.
- Key US advisers had accepted the model of a dynamic and expansionist communism that threatened US interests.

What were the results?

- The USA was committed to an active foreign policy of containment and to use its economic and military power to intervene in European and then in world affairs. This was in marked contrast to the isolationism that followed World War I and was to last well into the twenty-first century.
- The policy confirmed the emergence of mutually hostile blocs.
- It strengthened anti-communist feeling in the USA and the so-called **Red scare**.
- It also strengthened the hostility in the Communist bloc, which saw only US attempts to use '**dollar diplomacy**' to exercise power and bolster its existing allies. Aid went to 17 countries, but mostly to the UK and West Germany (which were not in danger of becoming communist), France and Italy.
- Most of the $12.7 billion in aid was used to purchase goods and raw materials from the USA, and considerable amounts went into defence spending.
- It supported the re-industrialisation of West Germany, which promoted its political stability after 1949.
- Economic results were variable. Britain did not use the opportunity for investment in infrastructure, for instance.
- There was a long-term commitment to aid, which continued after 1951 with $7 billion a year going to Europe under the Mutual Security Plan.

Introducing an argument

Below is a sample exam question, a list of key points to be made in the answer, and a simple introduction and conclusion for the answer. Read these and then, using the information on the opposite page, rewrite the introduction and the conclusion in order to develop an argument.

'The USA followed a policy of containment out of self-interest.' How far do you agree?

Key points

- The USA supported free people in their attempt to resist subjugation.
- Britain faced serious economic problems.
- There was civil war in Greece.
- The Yalta agreement.
- Communism had gained support in some Western European countries.
- US economic interests.
- Economic decline in the 1930s and the rise of totalitarian regimes.

Introduction

To an extent it could be argued that the USA followed a policy of containment out of self-interest. There were many concerns for the USA as the Yalta agreement appeared to have failed. There was also a civil war in Greece and Britain was economically weak. The USA was faced with growing popular support for communism in some Western European countries and was worried by that as well as by the need to promote its own economy.

Conclusion

There were many reasons why the USA followed a policy of containment. It was certainly concerned about its own interests, but the situation in Europe was also a problem for the USA. There were also concerns that an economic decline could lead to a return to the type of regimes that existed in the 1930s, and this would damage the USA.

 Turning assertion into argument   a

Below is a sample question and a series of assertions. Read the exam question and then add a justification to each of the assertions to turn it into an argument.

'The policy of containment brought more benefit to the USA than to Europe.' How far do you agree?

The US economy gained substantially from the policy of containment because...

_____

_____

Though important to the USA, containment was beneficial to the West because...

_____

_____

Most importantly, it created hostility in the Communist bloc because...

_____

_____

Cominform and Comecon

Stalin sent his foreign minister Molotov to meet representatives from France and Britain to discuss Marshall Aid proposals, but feared Western interference with economic policy in the East. Stalin banned Soviet bloc governments from accepting aid, and called a conference in Poland of all European communist parties, including those in France and Italy. From that, the Communist Information Bureau (**Cominform**) emerged in September 1947. The other communist organisation formed as a reaction to US policies was the Council of Mutual Economic Assistance (**Comecon**) in 1949.

Cominform

The Polish Conference was held to resolve disagreements in Eastern Europe about rejecting much-needed aid. From 1919 to 1943 there had been a central organisation to coordinate communist parties – the **Comintern** or the Third International. This had been dominated by the USSR. Cominform was intended as propaganda to prevent any communist party being lured by US 'dollar diplomacy'. The most enthusiastic party was the Yugoslav and its first headquarters was in Belgrade. Its aims were to provide information to strengthen 'the anti-imperialist and democratic camp, the principal aim of which is to undermine imperialism, strengthen democracy and liquidate the remnants of fascism'.

After the rift between the Yugoslav communist leader **Tito** and Stalin and the expulsion of Yugoslavia in 1948 Cominform moved to Bucharest, though the dominant influence was the USSR. The propaganda aimed to undermine the Truman Doctrine and the Marshall Plan in France and Italy, and to maintain socialist unity in the East. It was abolished in 1956.

Comecon

Politically, Stalin had established greater control in Eastern Europe, and the formation of the Comecon in 1949 was to create an economic alliance. Just as the Marshall Plan saw a link between economic prosperity and political stability, so did Stalin. The initial members were the USSR, Albania (left in 1961), Bulgaria, Romania, Hungary, Poland and Czechoslovakia. The DDR (East Germany) joined in 1950. In 1962 Mongolia joined, and Cuba in 1972, with Vietnam joining in 1978. Yugoslavia had links with Comecon. Unlike the Cominform, Comecon lasted into the 1990s.

During the Stalin era there was direct economic aid to Eastern Europe, but Comecon did not develop much in the way of regional cooperation between members. Economic life was dominated by relations between Comecon members and the USSR. In this it paralleled the operation of Marshall Aid. The Eastern bloc provided an outlet for Soviet manufacturers and a supply of raw materials. There was also a focus on developing industries to avoid the need for imports from outside the bloc. After 1956 more ambitious regional policies were attempted.

The principle of socialist economic planning was applied, ensuring that the different countries did not replicate industrial production but specialised on key products. It also promoted infrastructure development, like the international railway and electric power grid. Just as the USA supplied fuel, the USSR provided oil exports and later finance from a development bank (1963).

What was the significance of these organisations?

- Marshall Aid would have required a convertible currency and trade with the West. Stalin's control of Eastern Europe would have been threatened if Poland, Hungary and Czechoslovakia had accepted it. It forced Stalin into creating a division between East and West, represented by these organisations.
- Cominform emphasised Moscow's control of 'information' and the ideology of other communist parties. This strengthened the view in the West of a solid bloc of communism, which had to be opposed.
- Comecon helped divide Europe into two competing economic blocs. It boosted the USSR's control of its satellites.
- Cominform and Comecon were part of a reaction against US policies, which also included Stalin approving the communist takeover of Czechoslovakia, tightening of control over Eastern Europe and blockading East Berlin (see page 34).

Delete as applicable

Below is a sample exam question and a paragraph written in answer to this question. Read the paragraph and decide which of the possible options (in bold) is the most appropriate. Cross out the least appropriate options and complete the paragraph by justifying your selection.

How important were Cominform and Comecon in increasing Soviet control in Eastern Europe?

The establishment of Cominform and Comecon was **important/somewhat important/not important** in increasing Soviet control over Eastern Europe. Marshall Aid **supported/threatened** Soviet control and would have **required/prevented** trade with the West. Comecon also **increased/maintained/undermined** the USSR's control of its satellite states. Comecon and Cominform were also part of a wider programme of **resisting/upholding** US policies in Europe, and this led to the USSR **strengthening/maintaining/lessening** its control over East Berlin. The policy also resulted in the USSR **strengthening/maintaining/lessening** its control over Czechoslovakia.

 Identify an argument

Below is a series of definitions, a sample exam question and two sample paragraphs. One of the paragraphs achieves a high mark because it contains an argument and judgement. The other achieves a lower mark because it contains only description and assertion. Using the information from earlier in the book and the opposite page, identify which is which. The mark scheme on page 7 will help you.

- **Description:** a detailed account.
- **Assertion:** a statement of fact or an opinion that is not supported by a reason.
- **Reason:** a statement that explains or justifies something.
- **Argument:** an assertion justified by a reason.
- **Judgement:** an assertion that is supported by a fact or reason.

How far did Comecon and Cominform increase Soviet control in Eastern Europe?

Extract 1

Cominform was established in September 1947 and was followed by Comecon in 1949. They were set up in response to the US policies of containment. The aim of Cominform was to stop any of the Eastern bloc countries succumbing to the policy of US 'dollar diplomacy', while Comecon recognised that there was a link between political stability and the economy. Comecon provided direct economic aid to the states of Eastern Europe and was therefore very similar to Marshall Aid. The organisation also helped to develop industries so that materials would not have to be imported from outside the Eastern bloc, but later regional policies were also developed.

Extract 2

Comecon and Cominform played a significant role in increasing Soviet control over Eastern Europe. The Soviet Union was concerned that Eastern bloc countries, desperate for economic aid, would turn for help to the USA. Cominform ensured that no Eastern country was, in Soviet terms, lured by 'dollar diplomacy', which would have been a direct challenge to Soviet domination of the region. Comecon ensured that aid was provided to the Eastern states, but coming as it did from the Soviet Union it made those states even more dependent on the Soviet Union. The organisation ensured that there was a ready market for Soviet goods, while also providing it with raw materials, thus further developing the reliance the states had on the Soviet Union.

Conflicts over Germany, including the Berlin blockade and airlift

The creation of four occupation zones as a result of the wartime conferences and a joint Control Commission gave rise to conflicts about running Germany. A special problem was the division of Berlin, which lay in the USSR's zone, into Western and Eastern zones. As the two sides had very different views about how to treat occupied Germany, conflicts arose.

Tensions

Initially, the USA favoured a decentralised and deindustrialised Germany as in the **Morgenthau Plan**. But this was impractical and US policy changed. In mid-1946 there were talks between Britain and the USA to merge their zones. At Potsdam there had been agreement that Germany would be treated as a single economic unit, but the USSR's heavy reparations and failure to conform to the agreements made about exchange of goods and raw materials went against that. In January 1947 Bizonia was created from the US and British zones. In 1948 Bizonia ceased reparations and a policy of re-establishing a German industrial base began. There were also moves towards more German local self-government in the zone. The USSR for its part had encouraged a merger between the communists and the SPD and helped to ensure a left-wing coalition victory in the elections of 1946, making it increasingly difficult for other parties to operate.

Attempts at unity

Though neither side wanted permanent division, talks about unity failed.

Thus, in February 1948 a conference was held in London at which the USA, Britain, France and the **Benelux countries** met to discuss establishing a separate West German nation. In June 1948 Germans in the West were allowed to create a democratic constitution and a new currency.

Currency reform

The decision to create a separate currency, the Deutschmark, for the West was a key turning point. The USSR had not been consulted and responded by creating its own currency for the East, the Ostmark.

The key Russian aim was to prevent the creation of a West German state. Stalin chose to put pressure on the West's weakest point – West Berlin.

The Berlin blockade

In retaliation for the Deutschmark, Stalin imposed a blockade on road and rail links to West Berlin on 23 June 1948 and cut off its electricity. The Allies supplied the city by air. Each day 2000 tons of supplies were flown in and, as a threat, 60 B29 bombers were stationed in eastern England. The airlift was extended, reaching 8000 tons a day by February. The blockade and airlift ended in May 1949.

Who was more to blame?

The USSR could not afford to allow Germany to exercise political freedom, and the damage done to the USSR in the German invasion of 1941 seemed to justify reparations. The context of increasing Soviet control of Eastern Europe worried the West and the practical needs of restoring the German economy seemed to override possible dangers. Negotiating with the Russians in the Allied Control Commission had been difficult and there was little prospect of agreement over Bizonia or the currency issue, so unilateral decisions were taken that nevertheless seemed to be threatening, especially in the context of the Truman Doctrine and containment.

! Support or challenge? **a**

Below is a sample exam question that asks how far you agree with a specific statement. Below this is a series of general statements that are relevant to the question. Using your own knowledge and the information on the opposite page, decide whether each statement supports or challenges the statement in the question and tick the appropriate box.

'The policies of the Soviet Union were the most important cause of the division of Germany.' How far do you agree?

	Support	Challenge
Britain and the USA merged their zones to form Bizonia.		
The USSR wanted heavy reparations from the Western zone.		
Bizonia ceased reparation payments to Russia and developed an industrial base in its zones.		
The USSR encouraged merger between the communists and SPD.		
The USSR did not want a developed industrial region under Western control.		
The Western powers agreed to the formation of a new West German state.		
The West introduced a new currency into its zone without consulting the USSR.		
The USSR imposed a blockade on road and rail links to West Berlin.		
The USSR introduced its own currency for the East.		

i Turning assertion into argument **a**

Below is a sample question and a series of assertions. Read the exam question and then add a justification to each of the assertions to turn it into an argument.

'The introduction of a new currency into the Western zone ended any hope of a united Germany.' How far do you agree?

The introduction of a new currency into the Western zone ended any hope of a united Germany because...

_____

_____

Though important, the introduction of a new currency into the Western zone was not the most important reason because...

_____

_____

More important was the attitude of the Soviet Union to the industrialisation of the Western zone because...

_____

_____

The creation of East and West Germany

When France agreed to join Bizonia, this became Trizonia in April 1949. It was clear that separate states would emerge in East and West. Both sides had found political leaders with whom they could work. The experience of the blockade crisis had brought about increased division.

Separate development, 1948–49

The West approved the **Basic Law**, the constitution for the new West German state, in spring 1949, and elections took place in August. **Adenauer** became the new Chancellor but there was control of key areas of policy concerning foreign policy, defence and economic matters from a High Commission of the former occupying powers. The new republic was known as the Federal Republic of Germany and the pre-1933 political system re-emerged, with power being shared with the individual states. Bonn became the new capital.

In the East, there was more reluctance on Stalin's part to opt for an independent East German state. This would leave the richer and more industrial part of Germany, especially the Ruhr, in the hands of the West and he had little sympathy for any idea of German self-government. The official line of the now-dominant **SED** – a coalition between the former socialists and communists, in practice dominated by pro-Moscow Marxists – was that they stood for national unity. In 1948 they called on the National German People's Council to draw up a possible constitution for the whole country. This, however, was dominated by the communists. The events of the blockade made national unity unlikely and in May 1949 the People's Council approved a constitution. The elections offered the people of the Soviet zone a choice of candidates from the SED only. The People's Republic was a one-party state backed by a security apparatus that was more developed even than that of its Nazi predecessor.

Stalin delayed approving the formation of a new German Democratic Republic government until October 1949. A Soviet Control Commission mirrored the West's High Commission and exerted a great deal of control over the new state, although Russian occupying forces were withdrawn.

Berlin

Fear and dislike of the SED led to the establishment of a West Berlin city government and elected assembly in November 1948. Officially the four-power Control Commission ran the city, but West Berlin sent representative to the Bonn parliament though they had no voting rights. East Berlin became the capital of the new Democratic Republic.

The results of the division

- France and the USSR were unhappy about the creation of independent states.
- The USA and Britain, however, were deeply committed to promoting West Germany as a prosperous and stable ally.
- The USSR had accepted the division reluctantly, as the East was the less populous and economically developed part of Germany. Stalin remained uncommitted to an independent East Germany and was prepared to sacrifice it as late as 1952, when he offered reunification in return for a neutral Germany.
- East Germany became one of the most closely controlled, both economically and politically, and ideologically committed of all the satellites states. Its leadership was unhesitatingly supportive of Moscow.
- West Germany and West Berlin seemed to be a model of capitalist development and the great success story of the Allies – the Nazi past was put aside, there was an economic miracle and stable, conservative politics.
- East Germany and East Berlin remained impoverished, battle scarred and drab. Unification was increasingly unlikely.

Developing an argument

Below is a sample exam question, a list of key points to be made in the answer, and a paragraph from the answer. Read these and then, using the information on the opposite page and from page 34, rewrite the paragraph in order to develop an argument. Your paragraph should explain why the factor discussed in the paragraph is either the most significant factor or less significant than another factor.

'The most important reason Stalin opposed the creation of West Germany was because of economic factors.' How far do you agree?

Key points

- The Eastern zone was less populous.
- Distribution of industry and agriculture.
- Stalin wanted a neutral Germany.
- Concerns about West Germany joining NATO.
- The Ruhr was economically rich.
- Stalin's view of German self-government.
- Stalin wanted a united Germany.

During World War II the Russian economy had suffered. Russia wanted to obtain reparations from Germany because of the damage it had suffered during the war. The new West German state contained the economically richer areas and had a larger population than the East. The West contained the Ruhr, which was the most important industrial area in Germany. The West was economically more developed than the East. The Eastern economy was dominated by agriculture and was less advanced than the West. The West was therefore economically strong and had the potential to be very prosperous.

 Turning assertion into argument   **a**

Below is a sample question and a series of assertions. Read the exam question and then add a justification to each of the assertions to turn it into an argument.

To what extent did the SED oppose the creation of an East German state because of its support for national unity?

The SED supported national unity because…

_____

_____

However, in reality it feared West Germany's economic power because…

_____

_____

The SED was also concerned that West Germany would join NATO because…

_____

_____

NATO and the Warsaw Pact

In March 1947 France and Britain had signed the Treaty of Dunkirk, pledging mutual support in the event of a war against Germany. By 1948, however, fears about Germany had given way to greater fears about the expansion of the USSR after the seizure of power by the communists in Czechoslovakia in February of that year. In March 1948 the Brussels Pact bound Belgium, Britain, France, Luxemburg and the Netherlands into a pact for mutual defence against an aggressor, unnamed but obviously the USSR. There were agreements about broader cultural and social cooperation. The aim, however, was to get US support, and secret talks were held between Britain, Canada and the USA. The result was the North Atlantic Treaty of 4 April 1949.

This was partly a traditional treaty for mutual defence. There was an ideological element, however, as it was to defend not merely national security but 'freedom, common heritage and civilisation'.

The actual commitment was limited by the phrasing that each state could seek assistance in the event of an attack 'as it deems necessary' and the scope of action would be 'the area north of the Tropic of Cancer'.

There was to be 'continuous and effective' mutual aid to support countries' defensive capacity, however, and a Council with regular meetings.

NATO was like a wartime alliance. It also had distinct political aims. It was not a response to a similar organisation in the East – and indeed a parallel pact, the Warsaw Pact, was not created until 1955.

NATO expansion

In September 1949, it was learnt that Stalin had atomic weapons. In Asia, the communists took power in China in 1949. Then, in 1950, communist North Korea invaded the non-communist South. This led to the growth of NATO.

- NATO countries joined the Korean War to expel the North Korean invaders in 1950–53.
- There was the development of military agreements to standardise weapons and signalling.
- In 1952 the Lisbon Conference set up a permanent HQ in Paris under a Secretary General and a permanent military force of 35 divisions.
- The first major exercise was held in September 1952 and defence planning expanded.

The Warsaw Pact

The Warsaw Pact was signed on 14 May 1955 by the USSR and most of its Eastern European satellites (the DDR signed in 1956). Unlike NATO, it was not an agreement between independent states but a policy move by the USSR. It was a response to the entry of the German Federal Republic into NATO. It promised consultation on issues of mutual interest and assistance in the event of an attack on any one member country. Like NATO, it led to military exercises and planning. If 'a general European treaty of Collective Security' were signed – i.e. the reunification of a neutral Germany – it would lapse, indicating it was more a political than a defensive move.

Though it seemed that the pact divided Europe into armed camps, little had changed; Moscow already controlled the foreign and defence policies of its Eastern European allies. However, it did mean that if any of the satellites defected then the defence of the USSR would be threatened, so it strengthened the determination of Russian leaders to prevent any sign of criticism. It also meant that suppression of discontent would be by 'the Warsaw Pact' rather than by the USSR alone – a convenient fiction.

Simple essay style

Below is a sample exam question. Use your own knowledge, and the information on the opposite page and in other sections of the book, to produce a plan for this question. Choose four general points, and provide three pieces of specific information to support each general point. Once you have planned your essay, write the introduction and conclusion for it. The introduction should list the points to be discussed in the essay and outline the line of argument you intend to take. The conclusion should summarise the main points and justify which point was the most important.

How far was the establishment of the Warsaw Pact a response to the creation of NATO?

 Develop the detail **a**

Below is a sample exam question and a paragraph written in answer to this question. The paragraph contains a limited amount of detail. Annotate it to add additional detail to the answer.

Assess the reasons for the creation and expansion of NATO to 1955.

There were many reasons for the creation and expansion of NATO in the years to 1955. There were no longer fears about Germany, but initially talks began because of events that had taken place in Europe in 1948. The process was given greater urgency because of developments in Russia and China and the outbreak of war in 1950. NATO was created not only for mutual defence, but also for ideological reasons.

The importance of atomic weapons for the Cold War, 1946–55

The successful testing of an atomic weapon by the USA on 16 July 1945 and the destruction of two Japanese cities, Hiroshima and Nagasaki, on 6 and 9 August 1945 were significant for the Cold War. The USA and Britain had not shared atomic secrets with Stalin. The USSR was therefore vulnerable to pressure as the West had vastly more destructive capacity. Not until September 1949 did the Russians successfully test their own atomic weapons, which led to an **arms race** and the possibility of **Mutually Assured Destruction** (see page 52) if the Cold War developed into an unlimited war.

The potential to put pressure on the USSR was not taken advantage of. The USA was aware that espionage meant the USSR would catch up and develop its own atomic weapons. Official US policy was to work for international control of atomic energy, and in November 1945 it called for a UN commission to set down rules for control of weapons and to develop atomic energy for peaceful means. The USSR was suspicious, however, vetoing US plans for control and instead demanding an end to all weapons in December 1946.

The arms race

In practice, the USA went on developing atomic weapons. The USSR had the capacity and was helped by espionage, which provided Western secrets. On 29 August 1949, an atomic weapon that was a virtual copy of one of the 1945 US bombs was successfully tested in Kazakhstan.

The arms race intensified with the development of a hydrogen bomb by the USA. This produced a weapon in 1954 with the capacity of an explosion that was the equivalent of 10 million tons of TNT high explosive (the Hiroshima explosion had been 12,500 tons). The Russians tested their own thermonuclear bomb in 1953 and had a weapon the equivalent to that of the USA by 1955.

Espionage

The revelations that the Soviets had benefited from spies like the scientist Klaus Fuchs passing on atomic secrets increased tensions and also suspicions of communist infiltration. It led to the execution of two of those involved, Julius and Ethel Rosenberg, in 1953 and fuelled the anti-communist hysteria stirred up by US senator Joseph McCarthy.

Massive Retaliation

The USA had not used its advantage in atomic weapons and Truman had rejected calls by the US Army commander, General Douglas MacArthur, to use atomic weapons in the Korean War when US forces had been driven back. In January 1954, however, the US secretary of state, Dulles, had proclaimed what came to be known as the doctrine of Massive Retaliation. He argued that local defences would not be enough to prevent a communist invasion and that given 'the mighty land power' of the USSR, only a 'further deterrent of massive retaliatory power' would be sufficient for defence. In other words, the USSR should be aware that nuclear weapons would be used.

This intensified the Cold War and was based on a view that the USA was safer than the USSR from attack by aeroplanes bearing nuclear weapons because of its greater distance, as the USA could use bases in Europe and its planes could get to the USSR first. This encouraged the development of missiles, however, and also the idea of a pre-emptive strike, and so increased the dangers from a possible conflict. It also encouraged the idea that war would result in Mutually Assured Destruction – that if a crisis did lead to armed intervention and if nuclear warfare was employed to fulfil this threat, then both sides would face destruction.

Whether the arms race intensified the Cold War and endangered peace or whether it in fact prevented a war from breaking out directly between the USSR and the West because the dangers were too great, is open to discussion.

Spectrum of importance

Below is a sample exam question and a list of general points that could be used to answer the question. Use your own knowledge, and the information on the opposite page and the rest of the section, to reach a judgement about the importance of these general points to the question posed. Write numbers on the spectrum below to indicate their relative importance. Having done this, write a brief justification of your placement, explaining why some of the reasons were more important than others. The resulting diagram could form the basis of an essay plan.

'The main reason for the development of the Cold War to 1955 was the development of atomic weapons.' How far do you agree?

1   The impact of the destruction of Hiroshima and Nagasaki in 1945.

2   The explosion of a Soviet atomic bomb in 1949.

3   The development by the USA and the USSR of a hydrogen bomb.

4   The anti-communist hysteria of McCarthy.

5   Dulles' proclamation of Massive Retaliation.

6   The creation of the West German state.

7   The creation of NATO and the Warsaw Pact.

8   The Korean War.

Least important ← → Most important

Support your judgement

Read the sample exam question and two basic judgements below. Support the judgement that you agree with most strongly by adding a reason that justifies this judgement.

Tip: whichever option you choose, you will have to weigh up both sides of the argument. You could use phrases and words such as 'whereas' or 'although' in order to help the process of evaluation.

'The arms race and the development of nuclear weapons in the period to 1955 prevented a war from breaking out between the USA and USSR.' How far do you agree?

Overall, the arms race and the development of nuclear weapons prevented the outbreak of war between the USA and USSR in the period to 1955.

It was not the arms race and the development of nuclear weapons that prevented the outbreak of war between the USA and USSR.

Exam focus

Below is a sample exam-style question and a model answer. Read them and the comments around the answer.

Assess the importance of events in Germany in the development of the Cold War in the years 1945 to 1961.

From the end of World War II to the building of the Berlin Wall in 1961, events in Germany played a crucial role in the development of the Cold War. In particular, the Berlin blockade took the two superpowers, the USA and USSR, to the brink of war, brought about by the West's decision to create a separate West German state. Germany's geographical position in the centre of Europe only added to its importance and therefore its future development after the ending of the war was important, with the USSR in particular fearing its re-emergence as a major power, both economically and militarily.

> A clear view about the importance of events is offered. But the opening also explains the importance of Germany.

Germany's position in Central Europe and its potential wealth and military and economic strength ensured that neither side could allow it to be dominated by the other. Moreover, as tensions grew between the two sides, Germany was seen as a potential ally by both in the East–West struggle. As a result, the future of Germany was a key event in the development of the Cold War. The USSR wanted to reunite the country. It believed that the Communist Party would win the support of workers in both the Eastern and Western zones and take over the country, in the same way that the Soviets would extend their influence in other parts of Eastern and Central Europe. Not only was the West fearful of this, but there were also disagreements over reparations. The West took the majority of the refugees who had been expelled from former German territories that had been given to Poland and Czechoslovakia at the end of the war, and therefore wanted to delay delivering to the USSR its quota of reparations that had been agreed at Potsdam. The USSR feared that a united German capitalist economy would emerge and play a role in a US-dominated global trading system, made a greater threat by Western control of the industrial complex of the Ruhr.

> The fears of both sides are explained.

However, it was the decision of the West to merge its zones economically in January 1947 to form Bizonia, and its subsequent development into Trizonia with the later introduction of currency reform, that was the most important factor in the development of the Cold War. The failure of the 1947 London Conference over the future of Germany only confirmed that the reunification of Germany was impossible and that the creation of a West German state was the only option for the Western powers. The introduction of currency reform in the Western zone in June 1948, without consulting the USSR, led to the latter bringing in the Ostmark. It was this that convinced the Soviets of the need to force the West to abandon its plans for a separate West German state, and resulted in the Berlin blockade. The currency reform had made clear that two separate states would emerge and it was this fear – both economic and military – for the Soviet Union that would govern all subsequent decisions, particularly the decision to start the Berlin blockade.

> A clear explanation is given as to why currency developments were the most important factor in the development of the Cold War. Accurate knowledge of events is used to support the argument.

The Berlin blockade was important in the development of the Cold War as the East and West came close to actual war. The decision to supply West Berlin along the three corridors allocated to the West by the Russians in 1945 did raise the possibility of escalation in the growing Cold War, and there was even the chance of it becoming a nuclear war. The subsequent airlift to West Berlin made clear to the USSR how far the West was prepared to go to maintain its presence in the city and its unwillingness to back down in its decision to create a West German state. The ability of the West to supply its zone in Berlin forced Stalin to back down, but also added to the tensions as he had little option but to create a communist East Germany as a counterweight to the FRG. The success of the airlift not only ensured that the Western allies remained in West Berlin, but also that not only would Berlin remain divided, so would Germany and the continent. Therefore, although war was avoided, the blockade resulted in the division of Europe, even if that divide would not become physical until the building of the Berlin Wall in 1961.

The last part of the paragraph assesses the significance of the blockade in the development of tensions.

Although the tensions caused by the blockade did not lead to war, the ending of the blockade did not end tensions. The establishment of NATO, in response to events in Czechoslovakia rather than Germany, was a clear sign of the West's fears of Soviet aggression. This was added to by developments in East Germany, during the Korean war, and with the creation of a paramilitary police. Such developments only encouraged West German re-armament, which further fuelled fears in the East and would eventually lead to the creation of the Warsaw Pact and to the armed forces of the Eastern bloc having the same equipment as the USSR. Economic developments, particularly with the West German economic miracle and the availability of Marshall Aid, added to the division and played a role in the creation of Comecon. Therefore, although Germany was not the only factor in the hardening of division between the two sides, it was often the battleground on which the struggles were played out. Moreover, the growing prosperity of the West and its appeal to workers from the East led to a drain of skilled workers and eventually resulted in the building of the Berlin Wall, the physical symbol of the division between the East and West.

There is a balanced discussion of the role played by events in Germany and other factors in the Cold War.

Therefore, although events in Germany were important in the development of the Cold War and led, at least in part, to the breakdown of the wartime alliance, they were not the only factor, particularly in the 1950s. Germany was at the centre of the Cold War in the years immediately after the defeat of Hitler, and it was the decision of the West to introduce a new currency that was the most important event in the development of the Cold War. It resulted in the physical division of Germany and the creation of two new states, and led to the Berlin blockade – which took the two powers close to conventional, if not nuclear, war.

The conclusion places the events in Germany in the wider context of the development of the Cold War. It also reinforces the line of argument adopted in the opening paragraph.

The essay has a clear line of argument, although some of the paragraphs are stronger than others. This is a very large topic and an examiner would not expect everything to be covered. To reach the higher levels, however, it would be expected that the whole period would be covered and this is done successfully, with a balanced consideration of the role of Germany in the wider context of events in Europe and beyond. The judgement is consistent throughout the response and the importance of each event in the development of the Cold War is considered, which helps take the response to the higher levels.

Reaching the very top

Some of the paragraphs could have a stronger link to the question and the judgement. Use the comments and the mark scheme on page 7 to move the response to the very top level, making a list of the additional features that would enable the answer to achieve full marks. Remember, it does not have to be a perfect answer, only one that is a best fit with the descriptors.

3 The Cold War 1956–1984

The importance of revolts and unrest in the Eastern bloc 1956–81 for the Cold War: Poland and Hungary

The death of **Stalin** in 1953 encouraged hopes for change in Eastern Europe. Communism had shallow roots in largely agrarian societies, and the imposition of Soviet economic policies of collectivisation, and those of forced industrialisation and state controls that favoured the **USSR**, had caused resentment.

Poland

In Poland, there had been hopes that the so-called new course after 1953 might bring reform, better living standards and more political freedom. Poland's large Catholic population was unhappy about many aspects of communism; workers' wages and conditions were poor and farmers resented controls. The party itself was divided and after the death of the Moscow-dominated leader Bierut, the more liberal wing asserted itself and refused to accept Russia's nominee, Marshal Rokossowski, as defence minister. Hardliners could no longer count on the police and the army, and pent-up discontents emerged, with mass meetings and demonstrations and student publications calling for change. In October, party support went to **Wladyslaw Gomułka**, a communist leader, who had been imprisoned from 1949 to 1954 for 'deviationalist' activities. The Russian leaders criticised the Poles for anti-Soviet activity, but support for Gomułka grew in the so-called Polish October.

In the end **Khrushchev** accepted Gomułka rather than launching a massive invasion into Poland and Gomułka proved to be a limited reformer, loyal to the USSR and to the Warsaw Pact. The unrest in Poland was a major factor in similar unrest in Hungary, however.

Hungary

Hungary also resented Stalinist policies and the domination of a Stalinist leader, Rakosi, who was heavily dependent on repression. The condemnation of Stalinism in Russia weakened the leadership. Political rallies spread and on 23 October 1956 the police fired on protestors, leading to workers joining students and intellectuals in protesting. As in Poland, a previously disgraced liberal communist, Imre Nagy, took power. But Nagy went further than Gomułka, allowing non-communists into government and talking of

leaving the Warsaw Pact and Hungary becoming a neutral non-aligned country. The USSR invaded and the sheer size of the military force, with over a thousand tanks deployed, made resistance impossible. **Janos Kadar** was appointed leader and – after seeming to be liberal – imposed Moscow's rule brutally. Nagy was executed and some 180,000 Hungarians fled to the West.

The Hungarians might have hoped for Western help but none came, and the impact on the Cold War was surprisingly limited.

Why did the revolts have such a limited effect on the Cold War?

- The attention of the world was diverted by the British and French invasion of Suez in 1956 after the Egyptian leader nationalised the key routeway of the Suez Canal.
- The USA disapproved of the action of Britain and France, meaning that the West was divided at a crucial time.
- The scenes of repression by Soviet tanks shocked many, but as the USSR had accepted change in Poland there was still room for some hope for change.
- In the UN, most Asian and Middle East states abstained in a resolution calling for the Soviet withdrawal of troops from Hungary, so the West could not count on international support for any measures.
- The West had accepted the brutal control of the USSR over Eastern Europe and that had become part of an accepted view of the 'iron curtain'.

Consequences

Kadar made concessions after the repression that strengthened the regime. The failure of the USA to intervene revealed the limitations of **containment**. There was little long-term interruption of contacts between East and West. NATO was a defensive alliance and the West had already accepted that Hungary was part of the **Soviet bloc**.

! Spot the mistake

Below is a sample exam question and a paragraph written in answer to this question. Why does this paragraph not get into Level 3? Once you have identified the mistake, rewrite the paragraph so that it displays the qualities of at least a Level 3. The mark scheme on page 7 will help you.

To what extent did events in Poland and Hungary have an impact on the development of the Cold War?

Unrest in Poland was due to the lack of improvement in the living standards and the lack of progress in improving the conditions of the workers. Most Poles were also Catholic and they disliked the communist policies that were being implemented. Divisions within the Communist Party in Poland made it easier for opponents to assert themselves. In many ways the events in Hungary were the result of developments in Poland. As with Poland, the lack of liberal measures caused unrest and in both countries more liberal leaders were brought to power. In Poland the USSR accepted the change and the West hoped that it would do the same in Hungary, but instead tanks were sent in. Despite this, the West offered no help to the Hungarians and accepted the brutal suppression.

! Turning assertion into argument

Below is a sample question and a series of assertions. Read the exam question and then add a justification to each of the assertions to turn it into an argument.

Assess the reasons for unrest in Hungary in 1956.

The events in Poland were a cause of unrest in Hungary in 1956 because...

However, the Stalinist policies of Rakosi were more significant because...

In the short term, a major reason for the unrest was the actions of the police because...

The Czech Crisis

In January 1968 in Czechoslovakia **Alexander Dubček**, the new Communist Party Secretary, came into office, and in spring of that year he announced reforms that would introduce more democracy. This was firmly within a socialist system. There was no intention to abandon collective agriculture or state-owned industry or to leave the Warsaw Pact. The idea was that individuals would be able to fulfil themselves through socialism by having more input into decision making. The National Assembly would be able to discuss and decide issues relating to the development of socialism.

A key measure was the ending of censorship in June. The **Prague Spring** was a different kind of challenge from the open revolt in Hungary (see page 44), but more dangerous. Demonstrators in Warsaw shouted, 'We want a Polish Dubček'. The DDR leaders feared that Czechoslovakia would create economic links with West Germany. As freedom of expression emerged there were revelations about the crimes and repression of the Stalin era, which involved Russian officials. The ideas could easily spread into other Eastern countries and came from within the party.

The USSR faced demands from Romania to pursue an independent foreign policy and the influence of Chinese communism on Albania. Given that there were threats to its control, it became determined to stop further change in Czechoslovakia.

The dilemma of the USSR

As early as May, the Soviet leadership was contemplating intervention to keep its control over Eastern Europe. It had to balance the acceptance by the West of previous repression and the very limited chance of any help for the Czechs from the West, against the impact of an invasion on détente and on the image of the USSR as essentially peaceful. Invasion would revive fears and strengthen NATO, but ignoring the situation might lead to the weakening of Moscow's hold.

The invasion of Czechoslovakia

The Soviet leader **Brezhnev** expressed concern about the emergence of anti-Russian propaganda. Pressure was put on Dubček by talk of 'Czech revisionism' and extending Warsaw Pact manoeuvres in Czechoslovakia from July 1968 to early August. Dubček had agreed to control criticism of the USSR, but visits by the leaders of Yugoslavia (**Tito**) and Romania (**Ceausescu**) on 17 August made the Russian leaders fearful of a break-up of the Eastern bloc.

On 20–21 August 1968, 20 divisions from the USSR, Hungary, Poland, the DDR and Bulgaria invaded. The Czech leaders were arrested and taken to Moscow, where Brezhnev threatened them until they agreed to abandon the reforms.

The Brezhnev Doctrine

This was stated by the Russian leader after the Czech invasion:

> Each Communist party is responsible not only to its own people, but also to all the socialist countries, to the entire Communist movement. Whoever forgets this, in stressing only the independence of the Communist party, becomes one sided. He deviates from his international duty... Discharging their internationalist duty toward the fraternal peoples of Czechoslovakia and defending their own socialist gains, the USSR and the other socialist states had to act decisively and they did act against the anti-socialist forces in Czechoslovakia.

Source: Leonid Brezhnev, 25 September 1968

The policy was clear: the USSR and its allies, especially Poland and the DDR, would invade any communist country that deviated from its 'duty' as interpreted by the Moscow leadership. This ended any hopes of fragmentation or fundamental change, whatever agreements were made about arms or links with the West, and extended the Cold War until the USSR abandoned it in 1989.

Thus, while the Czech Crisis was arguably the most dangerous challenge to the authority of the USSR in the period 1953–68, it did not bring the Cold War any closer to ending but rather helped to extend it.

❗ Complete the paragraph   **a**

Below is a sample exam question and a paragraph written in answer to this question. The paragraph contains a point and specific examples, but lacks a concluding explanatory link back to the question. Complete the paragraph using the information from the opposite page, adding this link in the space provided.

How effective was the Soviet Union's handling of the Czech Crisis in 1968?

> The Soviet Union initially expressed concern about the anti-Russian propaganda that emanated from Czechoslovakia. At first the Soviet Union simply put pressure on the Czech leader, Dubcek, to control criticisms and this was given added force by the extension of Warsaw Pact manoeuvres in the country, which should have left the Czech leader in no doubt as to what could follow. This meant that when the Soviet Union became fearful of the break-up of the Eastern bloc, following the visit of both the Yugoslav and Romanian leaders to Czechoslovakia, it was easy for them to take action.
>
> _____
>
> _____
>
> _____
>
> _____

⦂ Develop the detail   **a**

Below is a sample exam question and a paragraph written in answer to this question. The paragraph contains a limited amount of detail. Annotate it to add additional detail to the answer.

How serious a threat to the Soviet Union's control of Eastern Europe were events in Czechoslovakia in 1968?

> The events in Czechoslovakia in 1968 were a serious threat to the Soviet Union's control in Eastern Europe. Firstly, there were concerns about the Czechs developing economic links, which could be a threat to the economic stability of the East. There were also concerns that freedom of expression would lead to critical ideas spreading. It appeared as if such events were part of wider criticism of Moscow. Although the sending of troops to suppress unrest might damage relations with the West, there were concerns that unrest could spread and therefore a variety of pressures were put on the Czech leaders, suggesting that the Soviet Union did consider the events a serious threat.

The role of developments in Germany in increasing tension between East and West: re-armament and the role of West Germany

The division of Germany raised issues about the role of West Germany in Europe. Was it to be a semi-occupied satellite state of the victor powers or was it to be a truly independent sovereign state? If so, should it have its own armed forces and should it be part of NATO? What guarantee was there that Germany would not once again try to recover from a humiliating defeat and assert its power in Europe?

Attitudes to Germany

The general view developed that the German people had been victims of Nazism as much as had those Europeans whom the Nazis had occupied and terrorised. As the Cold War developed it was seen as necessary to have the cooperation of West Germany. This was encouraged by the peaceful development of economic and political life in the Federal Republic.

Fear of communism

The Korean War was worrying for the United States and Britain. The East German leader, Ulbricht, supported North Korea and suggested that a similar action might be taken by the East. As the Federal Republic had no armed forces, it was highly vulnerable. On the other hand, the East had built up a paramilitary police force of 60,000. **Adenauer** asked the Allied High Commissioners to be allowed to build a defence force.

The EDC

A European Defence Community with a European army was suggested in 1950 by the French premier, Pleven. This seemed impractical, but a compromise was agreed that NATO would create a force in Europe that would include German armed units.

The idea of Germany re-arming was highly controversial:
- It reinforced the idea that Germany would become permanently divided and was opposed by many in the Federal Republic.
- It alarmed opinion in France, which feared future German revenge for defeat.

More independence for the Federal Republic

From 1951 to 1952 there were negotiations, driven by the USA, to establish a new relationship with West Germany that would make it an independent state and to begin re-armament. The idea of an independent Germany as a pro-Western buffer state against the Communist bloc was now a priority. In May 1952 a General Treaty replaced the Occupation Statute and removed the High Commission, paving the way for Germany to create armed forces.

Soviet response

The USSR responded by offering to support German reunification and the creation of a neutral Germany that would not join either the EDC or NATO. Little came of this, however, and Ulbricht was allowed to begin a more doctrinaire socialist policy in the DDR. This led to a major uprising in East Germany in 1953, with Soviet troops and tanks moving in to suppress unrest in June.

The East German rising led to greater support for a confirmation of an independent West Germany. Adenauer won the elections of September 1953 and the General Treaty was accepted by both the German and French parliaments in 1954. The French, however, rejected the idea of the EDC.

Re-armament and its effects

Germany could not remain defenceless, however, and in October 1954 France was persuaded to agree to a limited West German army and German entry into NATO, which took place in 1955. Germany was not to have nuclear weapons and British forces would remain there as a safeguard.

West German re-armament strengthened the division of Germany and also contributed to the creation of the Warsaw Pact (see page 38).

Support or challenge?

Below is a sample exam question that asks how far you agree with a specific statement. Below this is a series of general statements that are relevant to the question. Using your own knowledge and the information on the opposite page, decide whether each statement supports or challenges the statement in the question and tick the appropriate box.

'The increasing tensions between the East and West over developments in Germany were due to West German re-armament.' How far do you agree?

	Support	Challenge
The USA encouraged moves to make West Germany independent and allow re-armament.		
The West wanted West Germany as a buffer against Soviet aggression.		
A General Treaty in May 1952 replaced the Occupied Statute and began the process of West Germany creating its own armed forces.		
West Germany feared the build-up of a paramilitary police force in East Germany.		
The USSR was concerned by the development of NATO and allowing West Germany to join.		
There was unrest in East Germany, which worried the Soviets.		
West German re-armament led to the creation of the Warsaw Pact.		

 Introducing an argument

Below is a sample exam question, a list of key points to be made in the answer, and a simple introduction and conclusion for the answer. Read these and then, using the information on the opposite page and on pages 38 and 40, rewrite the introduction and the conclusion in order to develop an argument.

'How important were developments in Germany in increasing Cold War tensions in the period from 1949 to 1955?'

Key points
- The re-armament of West Germany.
- The creation of NATO.
- The Korean War.
- The development of nuclear weapons.
- The development and growth in espionage.
- The creation of West Germany as a buffer against the Communist bloc.

Introduction

There were many factors that were responsible for increasing tensions between the West and East in the period from 1949 to 1955. The establishment of two separate German states created difficulties. West Germany joined NATO and, as a result, was allowed to develop its armed forces. There were also developments outside Germany that increased tensions, such as the Korean War. The development of nuclear weapons continued and this was accompanied by increased espionage between the two sides.

Conclusion

Thus there were developments both inside Germany and elsewhere that served to increase tensions between the East and the West. Some of these were long-term clashes, which included the development of atomic weapons and the associated espionage. There were also events, such as the Korean War, that increased tension. The gradual development of two separate German states had caused difficulties since the ending of World War II and there was also the question of West German re-armament and of it joining NATO, which was a concern for the Soviet Union.

The Berlin Wall, its causes and consequences

The division of Germany produced, not the 'iron curtain' of **Churchill**'s imagining, but a relatively open front between the Soviet zone and later the DDR and the West. The steady flow of those leaving the East by 1950 had reached 187,000. In 1952, after appeals from the East German leadership, Stalin agreed to close the border, but a loophole remained in Berlin and emigrants used the city as a route to the West. In 1955 the USSR gave control of the border to the East German authorities.

Problems in East Germany

The problem was that the steady flow of emigrants – 3.5 million by 1961 – was causing long-term economic damage to the DDR. In all, 20 per cent of its people had left – including some of the best educated and trained, who looked to find better conditions in the West. This level of emigration left the population of those of working age quite considerably reduced from pre-war figures. The imposition of Soviet-style policies had hampered economic development in the East, while in the 1950s West Germany had experienced an 'economic miracle', with a developed capitalist consumer economy, reindustrialisation, trade links with the Common Market and US aid. The East faced continuing shortages and an old-fashioned economy based on restrictive controls and wasteful production.

Reasons for the Wall by 1961

From 1958 the East German leadership was considering greater controls, and by 1961 the opportunity arose when Khrushchev approved, and indeed may have suggested, closing the Berlin border.

- Railway construction that bypassed West Berlin meant closure of the frontier would not disrupt rail communication.
- The number of emigrants had been rising and in 1961 the numbers were high. In July and early August 1961 alone, 36,000 left via Berlin.
- Khrushchev needed to show the world – and the critical Chinese communists – that Soviet economic policies worked; and yet in East Germany they were obviously failing. Loss of skilled labour could not continue.

Ulbricht and his colleagues may have taken the decision on 12 August 1961. The frontier was closed that night and barriers erected, which then led to the building of a wall on 17 August. This divided the three zones of the Western allies in Berlin from the Eastern zone. A second, inner wall, was constructed in 1962 with a 'zone of death' between; this wall was strengthened right up to 1980. Some 5000 managed to escape up to 1989 and there were possibly 136 deaths among those attempting to escape.

The significance of the Wall

- The Wall was, in the view of the US secretary of state Dean Rusk, 'a monument to communist failure'. Its purpose was not to separate East from West but merely to keep East Germans from defecting. It was still possible for West Germans to enter the East.
- It led to a show of determination by the USA not to abandon West Berlin – US President **Kennedy** increased troop numbers and made a famous speech in Berlin in June 1963, pledging support and associating himself with the people of Berlin by declaring 'Ich bin ein Berliner'.
- It was a propaganda opportunity for the West as a symbol of oppression.
- It stepped up tensions between the USSR and the West.
- It confirmed the existing status quo in Europe and ended any hopes that détente or resolving tensions might lead to fundamental change.
- It showed that the communist leaders were now wedded to defence of a failing system rather than to resolving problems by expansion.

Develop the detail

a

Below is a sample exam question and a paragraph written in answer to this question. The paragraph contains a limited amount of detail. Annotate it to add additional detail to the answer.

How far was the building of the Berlin Wall due to the economic failings of East Berlin?

The economic situation in the East was particularly bad and was not helped by Soviet policies. On the other hand, the situation in the West was much better and could be used to show the failings of communism. This development also encouraged emigration from the East to the West, which had a serious impact on the East, particularly as numbers had been rising. It was essential for Russia to show other powers that its policies worked, but this was not happening. The East Germans were also concerned by the developments and were pleased when Russia approved the building of the Wall.

Support your judgement

Read the sample exam question and two basic judgements below. Support the judgement that you agree with most strongly by adding a reason that justifies this judgement.

Tip: whichever option you choose, you will have to weigh up both sides of the argument. You could use phrases and words such as 'whereas' or 'although' in order to help the process of evaluation.

'The building of the Berlin Wall did little to increase tensions between the East and West.' How far do you agree?

The building of the Wall helped increase tensions between the East and West.	The building of the Wall had little impact on the tensions between the East and West.

The first **arms race** had centred on building ever more powerful bombs. From the mid-1950s, however, the development of missiles led to a second and more deadly arms race.

The second arms race – missiles

The USA led the way in missile technology but by 1957 the Russians had caught up. In August 1957, the USSR tested a successful ICBM (intercontinental ballistic missile). This and the launch of its Sputnik satellite (see page 54) showed that Soviet technology was no longer lagging behind. Missiles transformed the nuclear threat. A successful missile strike could neutralise the launch of an enemy counter-attack and meant there would be little warning of an attack or any chance of stopping one.

The USA overestimated the number and quality of Soviet missiles and began a missile race, resulting in the Atlas missiles being operational by 1958 and the Titan and Minuteman being developed. In addition, greater flexibility was provided by the USA developing Polaris submarines equipped with missiles.

Mutually assured destruction

The USA shifted its strategic policy to an assumption that Russian attacks on itself or its allies would lead to 'devastating retaliatory strikes' with the capacity to destroy half the Russian population and 80 per cent of its industry. Thus, war would mean 'mutually assured destruction'.

As a response, the USSR developed more sophisticated weaponry that was capable of pre-emptive strikes in a much more targeted way. The MIRV (multiple independently targeted re-entry vehicles) warheads from 1964 set off a further race, as these more exact weapons would target US missile silos. The USA developed its own MIRVs and also defence systems. Thus, the arms race centred on:

- increasing the destructive capacity of missile warheads
- increasing the accuracy of missiles to attack specific targets
- developing systems to intercept missiles and to allow missiles to evade interception.

To prevent this getting out of control, further arms talks – the Strategic Arms Limitation Talks – took place in the 1970s (see page 56).

Star Wars

After 1980, however, the arms race started again. The new Republican administration of Ronald Reagan was suspicious of the USSR and concerned about the Soviet invasion of Afghanistan and also the expansion of naval forces. There was also fear of the power of the Soviet SS-20 missiles (in operation from 1978), which had multiple warheads. The USSR was concerned about better relations with the USA and China. The USA developed Pershing and Cruise missiles, which it stationed in Europe and, most significant of all, it developed the Strategic Defence Initiative (also known as 'Star Wars', because of its advanced laser and space-based programmes).

This went against the 1972 agreements to limit defensive systems. It was immensely costly and technologically demanding and put the USSR under a lot of pressure to compete, which was one of the factors that led to its downfall after 1989.

The unstoppable arms race

The arms race perpetuated the Cold War but prevented it from developing it into a direct conflict. It did, however, create a dangerous environment for world politics. It led directly to a crisis over Cuba in 1962, which came close to escalating into nuclear war. Efforts to end the race came from peace movements in the West and also from summits and talks. The pressure from technological developments and the mutual suspicion on both sides prevented these from being very effective, however. The arms race changed its character but did not really subside during the period.

Simple essay style

Below is a sample exam question. Use your own knowledge, and the information on the opposite page and in other sections of the book, to produce a plan for this question. Choose four general points, and provide three pieces of specific information to support each general point. Once you have planned your essay, write the introduction and conclusion for it. The introduction should list the points to be discussed in the essay and outline the line of argument you intend to take. The conclusion should summarise the main points and justify which point was the most important.

Assess the reasons for the continuation of the arms race.

Turning assertion into argument **a**

Below is a sample question and a series of assertions. Read the exam question and then add a justification to each of the assertions to turn it into an argument.

'The arms race perpetuated the Cold War but prevented it from becoming a direct conflict.' How far do you agree?

The arms race increased tensions between the East and West because...

_____

_____

However, in many instances it also encouraged peace movements and summits because...

_____

_____

But, on many occasions these were not very effective because...

_____

_____

The role of the Space Race in causing international tensions

The early 1950s saw considerable interest in outer space and science fiction in the USA, which reflected fears of communism and the infiltration of an 'alien' ideology into US life. Some US scientists were interested in space and atmospheric research and it was their initiative that led to an International Geophysical Year being set up for 1957–58, during which 67 countries contributed scientific research into the atmosphere. US scientists planned a satellite but in the event the Russian scientists, taking part in this international scientific event, gained the publicity for being first in the field.

Sputnik 1957

Despite a lot of research, it was not the USA but the USSR that made the first major advance into space, with the launch of a man-made satellite. The so-called Sputnik circled the Earth once every 90 minutes at a speed of 28,000 miles an hour. The USA became aware of this in October 1957 when the Russians put their achievements on show. These created a sensation.

● It seemed threatening that a Russian satellite was crossing the USA far in space – what if this were allied to weaponry?
● It showed that the USSR was technologically far more advanced than had been thought.
● It showed that Western liberal capitalism had not produced the levels of scientific and technological superiority that many in the USA had assumed.

This started a Space Race in addition to the arms race that was taking place (see page 52).

The Race

In November 1957 the Russians showed their technical advances by putting a dog, Leika, into space. The US navy's Vanguard Satellite launch failed in a humiliatingly public way in December 1957, although a more successful launch took place in March 1958. The USA formed the new National Aeronautics and Space Administration, using the rocket knowledge of the German scientist Werner von Braun. In December a US communications satellite, SCORE, was successfully launched.

These rapid triumphs were upstaged by the Russian Luna 1, which orbited the sun, and then by the most spectacular achievement to date, the successful orbit of the Earth by a manned spacecraft, Vostok 1, with the first astronaut, Yuri Gagarin. The first American in space, John Glenn, made a successful voyage in February 1962. The Russians achieved other 'firsts', with the first woman in space, Valentina Tereshkova, in June 1963 and the first spacewalk by Alexei Leonov in March 1965.

The Race accelerated and the USA decided on a costly and ambitious mission to travel to and from the moon. Kennedy made the element of challenge and competition explicit in a speech in September 1962 and spoke of a hard challenge, '[which] we are unwilling to postpone and which we intend to win'.

Both sides worked on daring projects – the Russians finally achieved an orbiting space station in 1971. In March the same year, a Soviet probe landed on Venus.

US achievement

Huge US resources went into the Apollo programme. This led to US astronauts circling the moon and returning safely in 1968. It produced one of the greatest moments of the century when Neil Armstrong and Buzz Aldrin landed on the moon in July 1969. The considerable resources taken by this Race and the efforts to control the parallel arms race by the SALT led to greater cooperation. The first joint US–Soviet space mission – the Apollo–Soyuz Mission – took place in 1975.

The nature of the Space Race

The Space Race led to considerable excitement about the possibilities of space travel, heroism, and technological advances that have not had the results contemporaries hoped for.

Turning assertion into argument

Below is a sample question and a series of assertions. Read the exam question and then add a justification to each of the assertions to turn it into an argument.

To what extent was the Space Race a triumph for the USA?

The Space Race was a triumph for US technology because…

_____

_____

However, in the early years it was the Russians who were triumphant because…

_____

_____

Moreover, the US achievements were also seen as limited because…

_____

_____

Recommended reading

Below is a list of suggested further reading on the Cold War, 1956–84.
- G. Swain and N. Swain, *Eastern Europe Since 1945* (1993)
- J. Haslam, *Russia's Cold War from the October Revolution to the Fall of the Wall* (2011)
- M. McCauley, *The Khrushchev Era* (1995)
- D.G. Williamson, *Germany from Defeat to Partition, 1945–1961* (2001)
- M. Bowker and P. Williams, *Superpower Détente: A reappraisal* (1988)

Détente and arms limitation

'Détente' is the term used for the period of improved relations between the USA and the USSR from 1969 to 1980.

Better relations in the 1960s

There had been summit meetings between East and West and some significant treaties had been signed. The Partial Test Ban Treaty of August 1963, the Outer Space Treaty 1967 and the Nuclear Non-Proliferation Treaty were signs that communication was open.

Reasons for détente after 1969

The USSR faced worsening relations with China. As well as ideological differences, there were serious border clashes in 1969. The USSR had plans for nuclear war against China, and even secretly asked the USA's reaction to the idea of a joint action against China's nuclear installations. The USSR needed to reduce its potential enemies. When Nixon visited China in 1972 and there was the possibility of better relations between the USA and China, this put even more pressure on the USSR to improve relations with the USA.

The USA also faced problems. The **Vietnam War** was costly. The sudden rise in oil prices in 1973 as a result of war in the Middle East made a reduction in arms spending seem a sensible policy. Concerns among the USA and its allies about the dangers of nuclear war would be met by arms reduction talks.

The Soviet leaders also faced economic difficulties, slow growth rates and problems in food production, resulting in a rise in food prices. Reduced arms spending would help provide more consumer goods and food.

Another factor that acted as a pressure for détente was the Ostpolitik followed by West Germany (see page 58), but by the 1970s there had been a big change in leadership. Stalin and many of the wartime 'old guard' had given way to more flexible and pragmatic leaders, like Leonid Brezhnev. Since the **Cuban adventure** in 1962 there had been fear of the effects of nuclear war. In the USA, the more rigid anti-communism of the Truman–Eisenhower era and the determination of Kennedy and Johnson not to be 'soft' on communism had given way to the more pragmatic – and possibly less principled – era of Nixon and his foreign policy adviser Kissinger, who based policy on national interest not ideology.

Détente and SALT

There were more diplomatic contacts, with Brezhnev and Nixon visiting each other's countries and agreeing in 1972 to outlaw biological weapons. The USSR and USA agreed the Helsinki Agreements in 1975, increasing contacts between East and West. Also in 1975, there was a joint US–USSR space programme.

The SALT treaty of 1972 followed talks since 1970 and established a 5-year freeze on constructing missile launchers and a freeze on ICBMs and submarine-launched ballistic missiles and long-range bombers. Both sides agreed to restrict anti-ballistic screens or defence systems to their capital cities and main missile sites. Leaving most of each country vulnerable in this way would, it was hoped, discourage any nuclear war.

In 1979 US President Carter and Brezhnev signed SALT II in Vienna. It was hoped the negotiations that had gone on since 1974 would culminate in permanent limitations of nuclear weapons. There was further reduction of missile launchers and MIRV warheads, but détente was to fall away and the US Senate refused to ratify the treaty.

! Support or challenge? a

Below is a sample exam question that asks how far you agree with a specific statement. Below this is a series of general statements that are relevant to the question. Using your own knowledge and the information on the opposite page, decide whether each statement supports or challenges the statement in the question and tick the appropriate box.

'The most important reason for détente in the 1970s was the improved relations between the USA and China.' How far do you agree?

	Support	Challenge
The USSR's relations with China were worsening, leading to border clashes.		
The USA was involved in a costly war in Vietnam.		
Nixon visited China in 1972.		
The rising oil prices made a reduction in arms spending a sensible policy.		
US–China relations improved following Nixon's visit, leaving the USSR more isolated.		
The leadership in both the USA and USSR was more pragmatic and put national interest first.		
There had been fears of a nuclear war since the Cuban Missile Crisis.		
The USSR hoped that by improving relations with the USA it would prevent a Chinese–American alliance.		

! Delete as applicable a

Below is a sample exam question and a paragraph written in answer to this question. Read the paragraph and decide which of the possible options (in bold) is the most appropriate. Cross out the least appropriate options and complete the paragraph by justifying your selection.

How successful was the policy of détente?

The policy of détente was **successful/mostly successful/a failure** by the end of the 1970s. Talks to reduce nuclear weapons took place between the two countries and treaties were signed **soon/fairly soon/some time** after the talks. Contacts between the two countries also **increased/remained the same/decreased** and this development was **helped/hindered/negated** by a joint space programme. The treaties signed by the two nations **had limitations/were far reaching** and **protected/left vulnerable** much of each country. SALT II, signed in 1979, was a further **success/disappointment** as it reduced missile launchers and warheads and the US Senate **supported/refused to sign** the treaty.

Ostpolitik

A key feature of détente was the process known as Ostpolitik (literally, East Politics) pursued by the West German leader **Willy Brandt** from 1969.

Barriers to better relations

The FRG Hallstein Doctrine stated that the Federal Republic would break off diplomatic relations with any state that officially recognised the DDR. The Berlin Wall had increased hostility. Any attempts at better relations would lead to fears from France of a future reunification and the re-emergence of a stronger Germany in alliance with the USSR. There was the additional worry of NATO opposition and the loss of US military, economic and diplomatic support. Brandt, however, saw that Germany could not be so relentlessly divided and was concerned with the economic costs of maintaining defences. His election as Chancellor coincided with more moves to détente.

Changes

Brandt signed the Nuclear Non-Proliferation Treaty in 1969, which the communist nations had also agreed to. He then began a series of complex treaties with the USSR, Poland, Czechoslovakia and the DDR, and also a treaty on Berlin with Britain, France, the USA and the USSR.

The key agreement was the Moscow Treaty of August 1970 between Brandt and Brezhnev.
- This agreed that neither had any territorial claim against any other state.
- It recognised the western frontier of Poland; Germany finally accepting the loss of territory of 1945 as 'inviolable'.
- The Federal Republic abandoned the Hallstein Doctrine and agreed that both Germanies would become members of the UN.
- Brandt did not specifically rule out future German unity or revision of frontiers.
- Brezhnev won recognition of the USSR-controlled satellite.

In December, a treaty was signed with Poland. The frontier was to be non-violable; ethnic Germans still in Poland were to be allowed to emigrate to the West and there were to be more trade links with and financial assistance from the Federal Republic. A treaty with Czechoslovakia was delayed but eventually signed in 1973, formally revoking the 1938 Munich Treaty that had ceded the **Sudetenland** to Germany.

The Moscow Treaty was dependent on reaching agreement over Berlin, and talks began in March 1970 with the four occupying powers. In September 1971, it was agreed that there should be no restrictions on travel between the Federal Republic and West Berlin, that West Berlin had links to the Federal Republic and that West Berliners had a right to visit East Berlin. The treaty did not, however, admit that West Berlin was actually part of the Federal Republic.

The Basic Treaty was signed in December 1972 between the Federal Republic and the DDR. The FRG agreed to recognise the existence of the DDR as an equal sovereign state and accepted that both Germanies would be members of the UN.

Results

The DDR had gained recognition of its frontiers and prevented West Berlin officially joining the FRG. There was no suggestion that the internal policies of the DDR should change or that the USSR would not continue to protect it.

Brandt had ended possible diplomatic problems involved with the 1955 Hallstein Doctrine (for example, the Arab States' recognition of the DDR as a reprisal for the FRG's recognition of Israel in 1965). It had gained concessions for West Berlin and had not weakened its ties with the USA or NATO. The way was still left open for some future reunification, even if that seemed unlikely without a much bigger change. It also opened the way for more talks in Helsinki in 1975 about reduction of armaments in Central Europe and human rights.

Support or challenge?

Below is a sample exam question that asks how far you agree with a specific statement. Below this is a series of general statements that are relevant to the question. Using your own knowledge and the information on the opposite page, decide whether each statement supports or challenges the statement in the question and tick the appropriate box.

'The policy of Ostpolitik was very successful.' How far do you agree?

	Support	Challenge
The Hallstein Doctrine was abandoned and both Germanies became members of the UN.		
Ethnic Germans living in Poland were to be able to move West.		
It was not agreed that West Berlin was part of the FRG.		
The Basic Treaty was signed in December 1972.		
The internal policies of the DDR did not change.		
The USSR would still protect the DDR.		
The FRG maintained its links with the USA and NATO.		
The borders of the DDR were recognised.		
The Munich Treaty of 1938 was revoked.		

Developing an argument

Below is a sample exam question, a list of key points to be made in the answer, and a paragraph from the essay. Read these and then, using the information on the opposite page, rewrite the paragraph in order to develop an argument. Your paragraph should try to balance the benefits against the disadvantages.

Assess the reasons why it was difficult to improve relations between East and West Germany.

Key points

- The building of the Berlin Wall.
- France feared that Germany would re-unite.
- There were fears that a strong Germany might ally with the USSR.
- NATO would oppose improved relations.
- The USA would remove economic and diplomatic support for the West.

There were many reasons why it was difficult for relations between East and West Germany to improve. In the Hallstein Doctrine, West Germany had stated that it would break off diplomatic relations with any country that officially recognised the DDR. In 1961 the Berlin Wall had been built and this prevented the movement of Berliners between the two sectors. A united Germany would have a strong economy and could ally with the Soviet Union. German re-armament was a worry for France and the military stability of Central Europe could change. West Germany relied on economic and diplomatic aid from the USA.

The impact of the new Cold War, 1979–85

The high point of détente has been seen as the Helsinki Agreements, but these did not prevent further developments in the arms race when the USSR stationed the powerful SS-20 missiles in Central Europe in 1976. The so-called new Cold War began, however, when Soviet troops invaded Afghanistan in December 1979.

Afghanistan

In April 1978, without Moscow's approval, the Afghan communists overthrew the monarch in Afghanistan and began a radical programme of secularisation and reform. This resulted in an opposition movement by Islamic forces with support in the countryside. The Iranian revolution had inspired the growth of Islamic radicalism and the USSR was vulnerable because of its large Muslim population in the southern republics. Already fearful of China and having restarted an arms race with the West, the USSR could not afford any more instability. It took rapid action, sending in large forces to the country. The communist leader Amin was removed and killed and replaced by Babrak Kemal, a communist loyal to Moscow. The Islamic revolt had got underway, however, and could not now be contained. The Afghan regular army fell away, leaving 50,000 Soviet forces to confront 200,000 Islamic **Mujahedeen** rebels. A long and bitter conflict developed that poisoned relations between the USSR and the West.

Western reaction

The invasion gave rise to memories of Czechoslovakia and Hungary and seemed to indicate that détente was pointless. There were fears of Russian expansion towards the Persian Gulf and the key oil supplies on which the West depended. President Carter banned grain supplies, the US Senate refused to ratify the SALT II treaty, and the USA boycotted the 1980 Moscow Olympics. In addition, the USA supplied the Afghan rebels through its ally Pakistan. By 1986 the level of aid included surface to air missiles. The USA also approved the export of Chinese military technology to the Mujahedeen.

Changes in leadership in the West

In 1980 Ronald Reagan was elected US president. He was openly hostile to the USSR and its 'evil empire', and saw the concessions in SALT as against US interests and Helsinki as a repeat of the appeasement of Yalta. In Britain, Margaret Thatcher, one of Britain's most ideologically driven leaders, was elected in 1979, determined to oppose socialism and communism and to support the USA.

Poland

Hopes that the Cold War might subside were also reduced when, after unrest in Poland (see page 72), the USA made clear its opposition to armed intervention by the USSR.

The arms race

The deployment of cruise and Pershing missiles in 1983 and the development of the SDI Star Wars initiatives (see page 52) confirmed that the new Cold War was to be accompanied by a new arms race. Afghanistan was a new **proxy war** and there was even a major crisis that threatened to begin a world war, when in September 1983 a Soviet warplane shot down a South Korean airliner that had strayed into Soviet airspace.

Why the new Cold War continued

For the Russian leaders Brezhnev (who died in 1982) and his successors Andropov and Chernenko, the Afghan War and the relentless arms race waged by the USA, together with tough opposition to the whole ideology of communism from the West, made ending the new Cold War difficult. The greater economic and technological resources of the USA, as demonstrated in the Star Wars developments, gave an advantage to the USA. This meant that it had little interest in reducing its favourable position by further détente. The Cold War was approaching its end game.

Simple essay style

Below is a sample exam question. Use your own knowledge, and the information on the opposite page and in other sections of the book, to produce a plan for this question. Choose four general points, and provide three pieces of specific information to support each general point. Once you have planned your essay, write the introduction and conclusion for it. The introduction should list the points to be discussed in the essay and outline the line of argument you intend to take. The conclusion should summarise the main points and justify which point was the most important.

Assess the reasons for the development of a new Cold War in the period from 1979 to 1985.

Turning assertion into argument

Below is a sample question and a series of assertions. Read the exam question and then add a justification to each of the assertions to turn it into an argument.

'The emergence of new leaders in the West was the most important reason for the development of the new Cold War.' How far do you agree?

It could be argued that the elections of Reagan and Thatcher were important because. . .

_____

_____

Their position was further strengthened by their economic and technological resources because. . .

_____

_____

On the other hand, there were fears over developments in Afghanistan because. . .

_____

_____

Exam focus

Below is a sample exam-style question and a model answer. Read them and the comments around the answer.

How effectively did the USSR deal with threats to its control of Eastern Europe in the 1950s and 1960s?

The USSR faced threats from East Germany, Poland, Hungary and Czechoslovakia in the 1950s and 1960s. Some threats were handled more effectively than others, however, and in the case of Hungary and Czechoslovakia excessive force was used, which built up long-term resentments. Thus a distinction could be made between immediately regaining control and longer-term over-reliance on force.

In two cases, those of the East German revolts in 1953 and the threat in Hungary in 1956, the USSR suppressed unrest by a considerable show of force and reinforced the authority of leaders loyal to the USSR. In East Germany, the authority of Ulbricht was reinforced and there was no repeat of the resistance to Russian domination in the 1950s and 1960s. In Hungary, the use of very heavy military power, with a thousand Russian tanks being brought in, ensured Russian domination. Here, there was a threat that the new, more liberal, leader Nagy might take Hungary out of the Warsaw Pact and make the country a non-aligned nation. This was firmly suppressed and a new pro-Soviet leader Kadar installed. Kadar followed the Soviet lead and Hungary remained both in the Warsaw Pact and a key element in the Soviet defence strategy. The Hungarian revolt was the largest and most serious threat the USSR faced and the very decisive military intervention sent out clear messages that it was not possible to offer resistance. It also showed that the Eastern policy of containment did not apply to lands that the West had already accepted would be part of the Soviet sphere. Though the USSR was fortunate that the West was distracted by the Suez Crisis, it rightly anticipated that there would be no Western intervention. 180,000 Hungarian refugees fled to the West but were not influential in changing Western policies and the invasion, though unpopular in the West, did not provoke major repercussions for East–West relations. In Hungary, Kadar – while not opposing Russian domination – did make more changes and

hard-line Stalinists were dropped and the new regime concentrated more on raising living standards and appeasing the people economically. This could be seen as a successful outcome, but the longer-term resentment about the loss of life, the shock of the execution of Nagy and the end of any pretence of fraternal cooperation between the peoples of the USSR and Hungary did shake the foundations of relations between the two countries. It was clear that the Hungarian regime was merely a puppet regime, that change would be difficult to negotiate and that Russian domination depended not on consent or ideological cooperation but just on force. When that force was no longer applied, control would be lost. The end of even the façade of consent to the alliance with the USSR and the laying bare of the reliance on force, even by a reforming government such as that of Khrushchev, was a long-term weakness that became evident in 1989.

> The focus in this introductory paragraph is on the threats; the USSR dealing with the threats and a view about 'effectively'. It is to the point and focused on the question.

> The focus is maintained on the effectiveness of the Soviet response.

> Some clear points are made about why it was effective, though there is not a lot on what the Russians actually did.

> There is some balance here, which engages with 'How effectively...?' and does not simply say in what way the actions were effective.

> There is a clear interim conclusion.

In Poland, there was a different policy towards the threat of internal change. The threat here was potentially greater. Poland bordered the USSR directly. Khrushchev, however, took a different line in accepting the apparently more liberal leader Gomulka after the death of the Stalinist Bierut. Given the concerns in the West about Poland, this was an effective policy that prevented any possible Western action. It prevented, too, a possible linking of unrest in Poland and Hungary and it actually resulted in a pro-Soviet regime, as Gomulka turned out to be considerably less reformist and liberal than had been expected and was a loyal supporter of the Warsaw Pact. The seeming concession, though, may have helped to provoke unrest in Hungary, but the USSR dealt with Poland perhaps more effectively than it did Hungary and Czechoslovakia, by achieving its main aims without an invasion.

This point could be developed.

There is a touch of balance here that offers some assessment; it is not very developed but there is a distinction between the different revolts.

By 1968 the changes in the USSR and the international situation had made Russia more concerned about internal unrest. The Czech threat was, on the face of it, much less than the threats offered by Hungary in 1956. The gap between living standards in the East and West had widened and the Eastern bloc was much less solid by 1968 than in 1956. If Czechoslovakia had succeeded in pursuing more liberal and democratic economic and political policies, there would have been a danger of this undermining the whole solidarity of the Warsaw Pact and the USSR's control of its satellites. Thus, on the face of it, the decision to use force seemed ineffective. Dubcek had no intention, in contrast to Nagy, of ending the Warsaw Pact. More liberal reforms might have paved the way for better relations with the USSR and might have produced more prosperity and decreased unrest. This meant that the Soviet invasion in the name of the Warsaw Pact again injured its international reputation, caused massive resentments within Czechoslovakia, weakened any loyalty to communism and paved the way for later changes in and after 1989. This may seem ineffective, but to Brezhnev the whole prestige of the USSR was at stake and so it was important to maintain control. There were fewer deaths than in 1956; in theory the Warsaw Pact as a whole was involved; and again there was no Western intervention (though much condemnation). In the short term, the power of the USSR in Eastern Europe had been reaffirmed. In the long term, the rigidity of the policies of the USSR had shown there was fear of change, which was to prove disastrous.

There is distinct judgement here, with a balance between effective and ineffective, but the explanation is not fully developed.

Given the threats, it is difficult to deny that the responses of the USSR were effective in the short term. However, in making it clear that the relationship between the USSR and Eastern Europe was based on military power and repression, it made it vulnerable later to the effects of weakness in the USSR and long-term resentment in the satellites.

There is a view here that is consistent with the opening view.

This is a strong answer that addresses the question and is generally analytical. It attempts to assess the effectiveness and so answers the question directly, and the understanding is good.

Reaching the very top

This is a good answer but it could be better. Using the comments and the mark scheme on page 7, make a list of additional features both in terms of explanation and supporting detail that would make this answer even better and reach the highest level. Remember that even an answer that reaches full marks is not necessarily the perfect answer, but one that fits best with the level descriptors in the mark scheme.

4 The end of the Cold War 1984–1995

Economic and social problems in the USSR and Eastern Europe

The end of the **Cold War** came when the **USSR** could no longer cope with the demands of global overstretch and a costly **arms race** with the USA, and so sought to revive détente with the West. An important element in changing policy was the economic and social problems of both the USSR and its Eastern European satellites. These led to changes, which weakened the control of the Communist Party both within the USSR and over the **Soviet bloc**.

Weaknesses of the system

Criticisms from within the USSR and hostile analyses from the USA suggested that the root cause was the weakness of the communist system itself.
- Planning objectives were unrealistic.
- The quality of goods produced, without the necessary competition between private firms, was poor.
- There was a lack of motivation in the workforce, as living standards did not improve.
- There were social problems like alcoholism and absenteeism.

This malaise had spread to the Eastern European countries, which were even more frustrated because they were closer to the more successful capitalist economies of the 1980s that were enjoying the freedom of deregulation from government control.

The USSR, however, had experienced both growth and economic success before the 1980s and when the West was suffering from problems with the rise of oil prices and rapid inflation after 1973, the USSR was more stable.

Stagnation

There was economic stagnation in the Eastern bloc by the 1980s. Growth based on industrialisation had reached its limits and further progress depended on technological innovation. This lagged behind the West. The agriculture and industry of the USSR and the **Comecon** countries had not modernised and there was a lack of investment. Too much spending had gone into arms production. By the mid-1980s the total production of the USSR was only 37 per cent of the gross national product of the USA.

The Eastern bloc suffered from a failure to stimulate economic growth by consumer demand as opposed to state-led investment. The two fundamental problems were in agricultural production and oil production.

Agricultural production

Agriculture suffered from a labour shortage as industrial and urban growth had ended the pool of mass agricultural labour. This had not been countered by better productivity. Attempts to exploit the land by increasing chemical fertilisation had led to serious soil damage. Heavy investment in irrigation had led to loss of resources – the Aral Sea had dried up, for instance. Basic food production, for example grain, remained stagnant from the 1960s to the 1980s, making the USSR more dependent on imports.

Oil shortage

The second problem was a significant fall in oil production in the USSR. The planned economy needed a regular supply of cheap oil. Also, the USSR exported 30 per cent of its oil, mostly to Eastern Europe. In the late 1980s oil production fell by 30 per cent. This hit exports and also damaged relations with the Comecon countries. The consumption of oil fell rapidly as imported oil was expensive. Oil had permitted an 8 per cent growth rate in the USSR in the 1960s – by the 1980s this had fallen to 1.8 per cent.

The whole basis of the planned economy was being undermined. The USSR was failing to deliver to consumers, to its allies or its defences. The infrastructure was outdated and this was dramatically revealed by an accident at the **Chernobyl** nuclear power station in 1986.

Economic and social unrest became increasingly apparent in the satellites, notably in Poland with the emergence of the radical trade union activity in the shipyards. Shortages and unfavourable comparisons with the more prosperous West were undermining the system.

Concept map

Make a copy of the concept map below and use the information on the opposite page to add detail to it, showing the economic and social problems of the USSR and Eastern Europe.

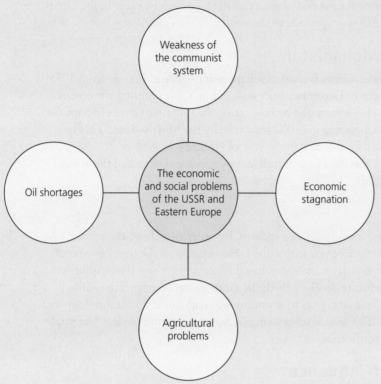

Develop the detail a

Below is a sample exam question and a paragraph written in answer to this question. The paragraph contains a limited amount of detail. Annotate it to add additional detail to the answer.

How serious were the economic and social problems facing the USSR and Eastern Europe by the mid-1980s?

The USSR and Eastern Europe faced many social and economic problems. These problems weakened the position of the Communist Party. The major problem was the weakness of the communist system. There were many problems and these had spread to Eastern Europe, where they created an even greater problem. However, the situation had not always been as bad, particularly when the West was suffering from problems after 1973 and the USSR was more stable.

The importance of Western influence and the arms race in bringing about the end of the Cold War

In 1985 **Mikhail Gorbachev** became the general secretary of the Communist Party in the USSR and began a revival of détente, which was a prelude to the ending of the Cold War.

Western reactions to Afghanistan

The West had largely accepted Soviet actions within its sphere of influence in Europe from 1953 to 1968. The invasion of Afghanistan in December 1979 was against a communist government but was seen as aggression, and the USA protested by boycotting the Olympic Games in Moscow in 1980 and more importantly by supporting guerrilla resistance by the **Mujahedeen**. This was more pressure than had been applied for instance in the case of Hungary in 1956 or Czechoslovakia in 1968. The USA also increased its military spending and extended the arms race, which put pressure on the USSR.

The arms race

Reagan rejected the previous restrictions on defence systems. By restricting these, the whole theory of mutual destruction as a deterrent was maintained. However, with the development of highly sophisticated and expensive new laser and space-based systems, there was the possibility that the USA could actually win a future conflict. With the ramping-up of defence spending by the USA, the USSR was put at a disadvantage as its economy was stagnant and its technology had not kept up with that of the West. The new, if unspoken, concept that a future nuclear war might be 'winnable' gave the West new confidence.

Limitations of Western influence

However, the pressure of the arms race must be kept in perspective.
- Soviet military spending was already high and did not increase in response to this arms race. The problem was that economic growth was falling and there was a shortage of oil. This meant it was difficult to keep up with arms production. It was this rather than just pressure from the West that led to Gorbachev seeking a way to scale back the arms race.
- The amount of direct pressure that the USA put on was also limited. Trade continued, as did exports of grain. Western capital was invested in the East. Reagan's belief in free markets and the economic needs of US banks and businesses overrode his ideological hostility to the USSR.

Wider world

The West put pressure on communist influences in the developing world. Reagan fought off communist influence in Nicaragua and invaded Grenada. These were more an indication of US determination than a major influence on the USSR. The aid to insurgents in Afghanistan, however, was more serious (see page 60).

Détente revives

The new détente of 1985–88 was an indication that the USSR was susceptible to pressure. In April 1985 Gorbachev stopped increasing SS-20 missiles stationed in Eastern Europe and he attempted at a meeting in Iceland to persuade Reagan to give up the SDI developments. He did succeed, however, in getting the total withdrawal of medium-range missiles in Europe at a conference between the USSR and NATO in Washington in 1987.

These concessions and agreements with the USA were accompanied by attempts to end conflicts with China. It was clear that the USSR needed to reduce conflict and military spending and to adopt a more flexible attitude to its economy (see page 68). It is possible that the main driving force was the internal situation in the USSR and its republics and satellites, but Western influence and the arms race were a contributory factor.

! Support or challenge?v

Below is a sample exam question that asks how far you agree with a specific statement. Below this is a series of general statements that are relevant to the question. Using your own knowledge and the information on the opposite page, decide whether each statement supports or challenges the statement in the question and tick the appropriate box.

'The most important reason for the revival of détente in the period after 1985 was US arms superiority.' How far do you agree?

	Support	Challenge
The USA increased its military spending, which put pressure on the USSR.		
Gorbachev was able to achieve the total withdrawal of medium-range missiles from Europe.		
Economic growth in Russia was declining.		
The USA had developed the SDI.		
The USSR faced a shortage of oil.		
The West was able to exert pressure on communist influence in Nicaragua and Grenada.		
The difficulties created for the USSR by the war in Afghanistan.		
The new arms technology was very expensive.		
There were problems in the USSR's republics and satellites.		

! Challenge the historian

Below is a sample AS exam question including an interpretation written by a historian. You must read the extract, identify the argument in the interpretation, and use your own knowledge to support and provide a counter-argument, challenging the interpretation offered.

'There is little doubt that the Cold War came to an end as a result of Soviet economic failure. This failure led in turn to a failure of nerve among the Soviet governing elite.'

Source: S. Ball, The Cold War 1947 to 1991

Evaluate the strengths and limitations of this interpretation, making reference to other interpretations you have studied.

1 What is the view of the interpretation?

_____

_____

2 What knowledge of your own do you have that supports the interpretation?

_____

_____

3 What knowledge of your own do you have that challenges the interpretation?

_____

_____

The importance of Gorbachev and his policies of glasnost and perestroika in bringing about the end of the Cold War

When Gorbachev became leader of the USSR in 1985, there was a widespread understanding in party circles that there were severe economic problems and a need to act to meet the challenge from the West. The two elderly leaders, Yuri Andropov and Konstantin Chernenko, had followed **Brezhnev** which meant that stagnation had characterised policy at a vital time. Gorbachev, relatively young at 54 and well-educated, introduced key changes.

Perestroika and glasnost

'Perestroika' referred to the restructuring of the economy to relax centralised control and to permit greater economic freedom and initiative. 'Glasnost' was an 'openness' that would allow more discussion of economic and political issues to drive progress. In 1986 state controls of the media were relaxed and the public learnt about the inefficiencies and corruption that had come to characterise national and local political and economic management. This was to be a prelude to new ideas and reforms to stop decline.

Political change

In January 1987 Gorbachev spoke openly to the Central Committee of the weaknesses of the system and he proposed much greater public participation and making officials more accountable. Multi-candidate elections by secret ballot for the local councils (Soviets) and party organisations were proposed. In June 1987 private enterprise was allowed in some industries. The changes divided the party. Some hardliners felt that this was a dangerous path when the threat from the USA and China was unresolved. Others wanted more radical reforms. The hold of the Communist Party began to weaken. New political organisations began to form, like the Democratic Union. Political criticisms in books and pamphlets appeared and more open religious worship once again began to emerge.

The changes did not lead to grateful appreciation of the Communist Party. The new private industries did not all prove efficient and long-term economic problems continued. There were more shortages than before of some goods, and the disruption to economic life caused some job losses and uncertainty.

In February 1989 there were elections for a new Congress of People's Deputies, which saw the defeat of many of the party establishment. New political leaders from outside the party emerged, including **Boris Yeltsin**. Although not intended to be a parliament, the new Congress came to assume that role. In 1990 the official dominance of the Communist Party in the USSR was ended.

The party and its authoritarian control had kept together a very disparate empire of Soviet republics and also controlled the Eastern European satellite states. When that control weakened, the empire fell apart (see page 72).

The impact of the changes

The pace and urgency of change were determined by the changing economic context and the external pressures of the new Cold War. There had been pressures for change in the satellites but these had been controlled in Poland. The existence of a reform movement – Solidarity – paved the way for reform, however. The similar problems of economic stagnation and corruption had been criticised in Hungary and Bulgaria and these countries were prepared to adopt similar measures to Gorbachev. In the DDR and Romania, the leadership showed little desire for change. Thus, Eastern Europe was divided over the changes. By 1989, Gorbachev would not bolster unpopular communist regimes that were unwilling to apply the remedies he had introduced in the USSR.

The end of the Cold War

Thus, integral changes in the USSR paved the way for a new détente (see page 56) and meant that instead of pressure for change being dictated by Western pressure, it was coming from the leadership of the USSR itself.

Simple essay style

Below is a sample exam question. Use your own knowledge, and the information on the opposite page and in other sections of the book, to produce a plan for this question. Choose four general points, and provide three pieces of specific information to support each general point. Once you have planned your essay, write the introduction and conclusion for it. The introduction should list the points to be discussed in the essay and outline the line of argument you intend to take. The conclusion should summarise the main points and justify which point was the most important.

How important was political change within the USSR in bringing about the end of the Cold War?

Turning assertion into argument a

Below is a sample question and a series of assertions. Read the exam question and then add a justification to each of the assertions to turn it into an argument.

'The domestic policies of Gorbachev were the most important reason for the ending of the Cold War.' How far do you agree?

The policies of perestroika and glasnost were the most important reasons for the ending of the Cold War because...

_____

_____

However, the military power of the USA was important because...

_____

_____

Yet it was not as important because...

_____

_____

The importance of the Soviet invasion of Afghanistan in ending the Cold War

In 1979, 100,000 USSR forces entered Afghanistan and installed a more controllable communist leader. They faced opposition to Moscow-dominated communist rule inspired by Islamic beliefs and supported by the USA via Pakistan. Soviet troops withdrew in 1989.

The problems of the war

The nature of the terrain in Afghanistan – which had created problems for European powers trying to control the country since the nineteenth century – led to a sustained guerrilla war. The experience of USSR forces echoed the US struggle in **Vietnam**. The opposition fighters had the support of local populations. Their religious convictions made them willing to endure casualties. The Afghan national army faded away and the forces of the USSR were engaged in a direct conflict with a ruthless enemy with years of experience fighting in the harsh and difficult terrain. The war was fought with increasing brutality and disregard for civilian casualties. The war damaged the reputation of the USSR not only in the West but also within the Soviet bloc, which saw it as costly – over 38,000 Soviets died or were wounded – and pointless.

The effects of the war

Previously, armed Soviet intervention in satellite states in Europe had been effective and short-lived. There had been limited resistance internally and the West had not acted. This was not true in Afghanistan and thus it eroded the confidence of Soviet leaders in using military intervention. Thus, military action was not seen as a viable option in 1989 when the Soviet Empire began to disintegrate, and this led to the end of the USSR and the Cold War.

The second effect of the war was it demonstrated the weakness of the Red Army. The army had supported the communist regime since the time of the Civil War. It had emerged victorious in the war against Hitler and had imposed controls over Eastern Europe. One of the assumptions of the Cold War was of a great Soviet military machine capable of invading Europe unless deterred by the NATO alliance. Its inability to defeat guerrilla forces, the increasing resort to acts of brutality and terror, and the disintegration of discipline and morale, combined to weaken the reputation of the army. For example, in September 1985 the execution of a civilian led to a mutiny by Central Asian Muslim troops in northern Afghanistan that resulted in 450 deaths and in 500 vehicles being destroyed. It was by no means certain that the army would be successful in maintaining control over breakaway republics or satellites, and this contributed to the collapse of the empire of the USSR. The failures in Afghanistan also changed the perception of the West and made the Cold War more 'winnable'.

The losses in Afghanistan increased resentment within the USSR from non-Russians, who felt that they were paying the price for involvement in a war that brought little benefit to those outside Russia and its leadership. There were protests about the call-up of troops from the Baltic republics, for instance, and '**draft dodging**' became common.

Public awareness of the war

It was difficult to impose censorship on the lack of success. When glasnost allowed press freedom, the reporting of the war brought about discontent and a demand for political change. The veterans of the war – the *Afghanisti* – provided a lot of criticism of the ruling communist elites and were active in political opposition. In addition, the spiralling costs of the war were another drain on a Russian economy already having to meet heavier defence demands and to import more wheat and oil.

Develop the detail **a**

Below is a sample exam question and a paragraph written in answer to this question. The paragraph contains a limited amount of detail. Annotate it to add additional detail to the answer.

How important were events in Afghanistan in ending the Cold War?

> The invasion and war in Afghanistan had a serious impact on both the Soviet military and the economy. In previous conflicts the Soviets had been able to secure a quick victory, but this did not happen in Afghanistan. This had a serious impact on the attitude of the Soviet military as it showed that the army was weak and had an impact on its attitude towards the Eastern bloc. The war also caused resentment within the Soviet Union and this was added to by the press.

Use your own knowledge to support or contradict **a**

Below is an interpretation about the impact of the Afghan war on the Soviet Union. You are asked to summarise the interpretation, then use your own knowledge to agree with it and then to contradict it.

The repeated failures in this war changed the Soviet leadership's perception of the effectiveness of using force to keep non-Soviet nationalities within the Union and devastated the morale and legitimacy of the army. War failures weakened the military and conservative anti-reform forces and accelerated glasnost and perestroika. Importantly, these failures demonstrated that the Soviet army was not invincible, thereby encouraging non-Russian republics to push for independence with little fear of a military backlash.

Adapted from: R. Reuveny and A. Prakash, The Afghanistan War and the Breakdown of the Soviet Union *(1999)*

- Summary:

_____

_____

- Agree with the interpretation:

_____

_____

- Contradict the interpretation:

_____

_____

_____

The events of 1989 in Eastern Europe

In Poland, Hungary and Bulgaria there was internal change with the acceptance of Gorbachev, which ended the communist monopoly of power. This led to the rapid spread of political change in the East. The end of the USSR's control of its satellites paved the way for the end of the USSR itself in 1991 and of the Cold War.

Poland

Economic unrest, including strikes in the shipyards of Gdansk in 1988, led the government to recognise the Solidarity movement. In April 1989 the Round Table Agreements saw Solidarity recognised as a political party. There was a new constitution, with Solidarity allowed to compete with the Communist Party for 35 per cent of the seats in a lower house of parliament. There would be free elections for the second chamber and both houses would elect a president. The elections of June resulted in a Solidarity government with some Communists holding major posts.

The existing leader, Jaruzelski, remained president, and Communists held key posts in the new government. Poland remained part of the Warsaw Pact, but the USSR had accepted a non-Communist government and important constitutional change.

Hungary

Unrest in 1988 resulted in the replacement of **Kadar** by a reforming communist, Grosz, who planned in 1989 to introduce a multi-party system. It was agreed with opposition groups to hold free elections in 1990.

Bulgaria

The veteran communist leader Zhivkov was removed from power in November 1989 by the reforming foreign minister Mladenov. Talks were held with opposition groups for free elections in 1990.

The DDR

Hungary opened its borders with Austria in August 1989. This made it possible for 150,000 East Germans to leave for the West via this route. There were demonstrations in Leipzig in September and October 1989 calling for change. The East German leader Honecker could not count on Gorbachev, who advised him to make changes.

Berlin

Crowds were growing in major cities, with half a million in East Berlin demanding reform and freedom to travel. The government allowed free exit from 10 November 1989, but as soon as this was announced on the 9th the border guards opened up crossing points from East to West Berlin, effectively opening the Berlin Wall. The Wall was subsequently torn down by crowds.

Czechoslovakia

News from Berlin led to large-scale demonstrations for political changes to match the economic changes already made by the communist regime. Opposition groups, including the famous Charter 77 group led by the dramatist Vaclav Havel, formed an organisation called Civic Forum and demanded change. They formed a coalition government in December in which the Communists were only a minority, and Havel was made president. The so-called 'Velvet Revolution' led to the end of communism and the formation of two states, Slovakia and the Czech Republic, in 1992.

Romania

Demonstrations against President **Ceausescu** began in the city of Timisoara in November 1989, influenced by events in Hungary, and then spread. Ceausescu and his wife fled but were captured and executed on 25 December 1989 – the only leaders to suffer this fate. Opposition groups formed a coalition and a new leader, Ion Illescu, was elected.

Common elements in the events of 1989

- A build-up of resentment against a background of economic underperformance and rising prices.
- Reforming leaders and groups who were ready to share power.
- The acceptance by Gorbachev and the Moscow leadership that states outside the USSR should make changes and an unwillingness to use force to maintain the Brezhnev Doctrine.
- Widespread popular support for change.
- Rapid arrangements for free elections.

Support your judgement   a

Read the sample exam question and two basic judgements below. Support the judgement that you agree with most strongly by adding a reason that justifies this judgement.

Tip: whichever option you choose, you will have to weigh up both sides of the argument. You could use phrases and words such as 'whereas' or 'although' in order to help the process of evaluation.

How far were the political changes in Eastern Europe in 1989 due to reforming leaders?

> Reforming leaders were important in bringing about political change in Eastern Europe because...
>
> _____
>
> _____
>
> _____
>
> _____

> Popular support for change was the most important factor in bringing about political change because...
>
> _____
>
> _____
>
> _____
>
> _____

Developing an argument

Below is a sample exam question, a list of key points to be made in the answer, and a paragraph from the essay. Read these and then, using the information on the opposite page, rewrite the paragraph in order to develop an argument. Your paragraph should explain why the factor discussed in the paragraph is either the most significant factor or less significant than another factor.

Communist power collapsed in Eastern Europe because of economic problems in the Eastern bloc. How far do you agree?

Key points

- Support for Gorbachev
- Economic problems
- Free elections
- Reforming communist leaders
- Popular support for change
- Demonstrations
- Events in Berlin.

> Economic problems in the Eastern bloc states created disquiet among a large part of the populations. The government in Poland recognised Solidarity because of economic unrest and strikes, particularly in the shipyards of Gdansk. There were also communist leaders in Poland, Hungary and Bulgaria who were willing to consider reform and allow free elections. There was popular support for change, and large-scale demonstrations in cities such as Berlin and Leipzig put pressure on governments. Some governments took action to prevent unrest, with Hungary opening its borders and free exit being allowed from East Berlin after 10 November. News of these developments spread to other states, such as Czechoslovakia.

The coup of 1991 and Russia under Yeltsin

The coup

The rapid changes since 1989 had built up opposition from conservative elements in the Communist Party and from some of the leading figures in government, the army and the KGB. A proposal to reform the Soviet Union by a New Union Treaty led to an attempted takeover of the state, beginning on 19 August. Troops took control of the TV and radio stations in Moscow and moved into the capital. Gorbachev was detained in the Crimea and cut off from all links with Moscow. Had the coup succeeded then resistance from the Baltic states might well have been met with considerable armed force, with the Communist Party reinforced and considerable repression of opinion imposed within the USSR. The Cold War might have restarted, with the good relations that Gorbachev had established with the West overturned. US President Bush pleaded directly with the plotters. The opposition of the President Boris Yeltsin, a popular figure in Moscow, however, was a key element in the failure of the coup. Yeltsin made an emotional appeal, in which he jumped on a tank. The tide had turned by 21 August and the troops were withdrawn. Gorbachev was restored and the plotters, condemned by the parliament, fled.

The détente with the West had been preserved but the aftermath of the coup confirmed the end of the Cold War because it led to significant developments that weakened the former USSR.

Yeltsin

Gorbachev was discredited and Yeltsin became the dominant leader until Gorbachev finally resigned in 1991. Unstable and with poor judgement, Yeltsin saw off the Communist Party, banning it from political activities in November 1991, and accepted the break-up and formal demise of the USSR. The Baltic republics took advantage of the coup to leave the union. Yeltsin, apparently in a state of intoxication, accepted the withdrawal of Russia, Belarus and Ukraine in December 1991. In effect, the largest state had seceded from the union and the controlling, unifying influence of the Communist Party was removed.

Economic change and problems

Yeltsin launched a sudden transformation to a capitalist, individualistic culture. State controls and welfare were removed. Trade was liberalised, state industries were privatised, and agriculture was deregulated. To avoid massive inflation, there were very high interest rates and high taxes in an austerity programme. The effects were devastating:

- Massive inflation wiped out savings and threw those on fixed incomes into poverty.
- There was a catastrophic decline in production and GDP halved.
- Infrastructure and investment declined.
- Subsidies were withdrawn and welfare slashed, leaving intense poverty and limited demand so that a consumer-based economy was slow to develop.
- Yeltsin faced such shortage of revenue that he was reduced to doing deals with a small number of powerful businessmen (oligarchs).

Social problems

Socially, there were disturbing signs of crime, alcoholism, inequality of wealth and lack of confidence or hope. Politically, the changes led to Yeltsin's unpopularity and the growth of ultra-nationalist and communist opposition. A low point was the tank attack on the Russian White House in 1993. Pro-communist army leaders brought tanks up to the Russian parliament building. The deputies, however, refused to accept the president's dissolution of parliament and openly defied the show of force, Yeltsin himself climbing up on a tank to make a defiant speech.

Weaknesses by 1995

A new constitution gave Yeltsin greater powers in 1993, but the brutal war against Chechen separatism that began in 1994 indicated old attitudes remained. This violence did not lead to any break with the West, however. Russia's newfound capitalism and adoption of Western economic values was seen as the final end to the Cold War because the underlying ideological split that had emerged in 1917 was now clearly over.

Eliminate irrelevance

Below is a sample exam question and a paragraph written in answer to this question. Read the paragraph and, using the information from the opposite page, identify parts of the answer that are not directly relevant to the question. Draw a line through the information that is irrelevant and justify your deletions in the margin.

Assess the view that the coup of 1991 stood little chance of success.

Gorbachev had introduced significant changes since 1989 and these had created opposition from many conservative elements within the Communist Party. Gorbachev had introduced polices of perestroika and glasnost, which restricted the economy and relaxed central control, allowing more economic freedom and openness to discuss economic and political issues. There was considerable opposition to the policies of perestroika and glasnost among important and powerful elements within the Communist Party, such as the army and KGB. It was the strength of support in the army that allowed it to seize the TV and radio stations in Moscow. The army was also able to seize Gorbachev while he was on holiday in Crimea and was cut off from all links with Moscow. If this coup had succeeded, it is likely that all the improvement in relations between the East and West that had been achieved by Gorbachev would have ended and the Cold War restarted. However, the actions of Boris Yeltsin ensured that, despite the apparent strength of the plotters, the coup failed.

Challenge the historian

Below is a sample AS exam question including an interpretation written by a historian. You must read the extract, identify the argument in the interpretation, and use your own knowledge to support and provide a counter-argument, challenging the interpretation offered.

'The coup [of August 1991] was defeated by a combination of indecision among the plotters, the resistance of ordinary people, and the reluctance of the security forces to support the coup.'

Source: R. Wolfson and J. Laver, European History 1890–1990

Evaluate the strengths and limitations of this interpretation, making reference to other interpretations you have studied.

1 What is the view of the interpretation?

_____

_____

2 What knowledge of your own do you have that supports the interpretation?

_____

_____

3 What knowledge of your own do you have that challenges the interpretation?

_____

_____

The reunification of Germany

The events of 1989 and the end of the Wall and travel restrictions between East and West Berlin opened the way for reunification. The withdrawal of support for the DDR from the USSR was a key factor.

Change in the DDR

The DDR accepted multi-party free elections, which ended communist rule. These returned a coalition led by a CDU politician, Lothar de Maiziere, in March 1990. Rapid reunification was driven by the economic collapse in the East and the devaluation of the currency.

The stages of reunification

The first step was a social, economic and monetary union in May 1990. To allow the DDR to function, the Federal Deutschmark became the official currency. That necessitated that West German laws should also apply in the East.

The East German parliament voted for accession to the West. The fastest way for this to happen legally was for the Federal Republic to accept more states, as it could under the **Basic Law**. As a result of the Reunification Treaty of 31 August 1990, the five states of the former Germany that had actually lost their separate status in 1952 agreed to join the Federal Republic, which accepted them as members. Thus Brandenburg, Mecklenburg Vorpommen, Saxony, Saxony-Anhalt and Thuringia – rather than East Germany as a whole – became official states or *Lander* within the Federal Republic.

Legally, Berlin was still under the control of the Allied Control Council set up after 1945. Thus, the four occupying powers of the Cold War period had to formally agree in October that Berlin should be part of the Federal Republic. This was formalised by the 'Two Plus Four Treaty', i.e. the two Germanys together with the four occupying powers.

In November 1990, the enlarged Germany signed a treaty with Poland guaranteeing that the frontiers of 1945 would not be revised. The new Germany became part of NATO – something urged by the USA – and the last vestiges of the Cold War ended with the withdrawal of the last allied troops in 1994.

The importance of reunification

The Cold War had ensured that Germany had not been able to dominate Central Europe, change the boundaries of 1945 or attempt to dominate its neighbours, as it had done in 1914 and 1939. It had prevented the rise of right-wing nationalism and tied Germany to different forms of democracy – parliamentary in the West and social democracy in the East. The militarism and dominance of Prussia, its army and monarchy, had not re-emerged. Both East and West Germany had been part of wider organisations that had controlled any possible attempts at revenge or reassertion of pre-war power.

The end of the Cold War re-awakened fears of Germany. Poles were anxious about the possible revision of their western frontier. The British leader Thatcher and the French president Mitterrand both expressed opposition and concern. Israel condemned reunification outright. It might have been expected that the USSR would be the country most opposed after its terrible experiences, but Gorbachev did not oppose it. The acceptance in Europe of a major change in the balance of power was remarkable. Cooperation in NATO and the European Economic Community, together with US support for reunification, paved the way.

The reunification was an important result of the end of the Cold War. For the people of Germany there was a painful period of readjustment. The West put in $2 trillion to the East but this could not prevent continuing inequalities. Unemployment remained much higher in the East and living standards lower. It proved more difficult than expected to reconcile the differences between the two.

Develop the detail

Below is a sample exam question and a paragraph written in answer to this question. The paragraph contains a limited amount of detail. Annotate it to add additional detail to the answer.

Assess the impact of the reunification of Germany.

> The reunification of Germany was very significant. The division of Germany had kept it weak and prevented its dominance, which it had exerted in the past. Politically, the division had prevented the rise of extremism and resulted in democracy. Prussian power had also been prevented by the division from re-emerging. The two states had also been members of various organisations, which had prevented them from pursuing policies of revenge. It was possible that all of these issues could re-emerge now that the country was reunited.

Spectrum of importance

Below is a sample exam question and a list of general points that could be used to answer the question. Use your own knowledge and the information on the opposite page to reach a judgement about the importance of these general points to the question posed. Write numbers on the spectrum below to indicate their relative importance. Having done this, write a brief justification of your placement, explaining why some of the factors were more important than others. The resulting diagram could form the basis of an essay plan.

How united was Germany after reunification?

1 Economic and monetary union, May 1990

2 Reunification Treaty, August 1990

3 Berlin

4 Germany joins NATO

5 Allied troops withdraw, 1994

6 Attitudes of Thatcher, Mitterrand and Israel

7 Attitude of Gorbachev

8 Unemployment and living standards.

Least important ←————————————————————————→ Most important

Civil war and the break-up of Yugoslavia

Yugoslavia had been the key area of Eastern Europe not dominated by the USSR. It had broken away from the Soviet sphere in 1948 under its leader, the wartime communist resistance chief **Tito.** The communist regime was a unifying factor in the country, but Tito kept Yugoslavia neutral in the Cold War. It became a member of the **Non-Aligned Movement** in 1961. Thus the end of the Cold War meant that its influence declined, as did its importance to the West.

Existing divisions

There was a history of violent hostility between the different national groups that made up the country. Yugoslavia was an artificial construction of the post-World War I treaties. Former territories of the Austrian Empire, Bosnia-Herzegovina, Slovenia and Croatia were joined to Serbia, whose king ruled the new state. Occupied by the Germans during World War II, anti-Serbian groups, especially the Croats, fought a bloodthirsty civil war against the Serb resistance to the Germans. The country was divided not only on ethnic but also on religious grounds, with a large Muslim minority.

The impact of changes in Europe after 1989

Tito managed to unite the country until his death in 1980. In 1989, changes threatened the hard-won stability. The USA was less committed to supporting Yugoslavia economically now that it was no longer needed as a counterweight to the Soviet bloc, which had collapsed. The ending of the power and influence of the USSR in the East removed a key element that had kept the different elements in Yugoslavia together – the fear of Russia. The unification of Germany and the break-away of the Baltic states, together with the growth of nationalism in other areas of the former Soviet Empire, encouraged nationalism.

Nationalism and the break-up of Yugoslavia

In Serbia, **Slobodan Milošević,** who became president in 1989, rose to prominence by promoting Serbian nationalism. His personal ambitions led to Serbia ending the autonomous status of the provinces of Vojvodina and Kosovo and to having his supporters established in Montenegro.

A similar process took place in Yugoslavia as in other Eastern European states, with free elections, the emergence of new non-communist parties and leaders, and economic changes. Elections in Slovenia and Croatia led to separatist demands for an end to the federal state and for a confederation of self-governing republics. Slovenia voted for independence in late 1990 and Croatia in May 1991. Both declared independence on 25 June 1991.

There was a substantial Serb minority in Croatia who wanted to join Serbia. Civil war broke out, with Milošević using the federal army to support the Croatian Serbs.

In Bosnia-Herzegovina there was further division and a referendum, which resulted in a call for independence being boycotted by the Serbs who lived there. Ethnic conflicts united with religious divisions. Despite international recognition of the separate states, bloody conflict broke out and there was some of the most brutal fighting and ethnic cleansing by the Serbs seen in Europe since 1945.

Continuing violence and intervention

This led to international intervention, which proved ineffective in protecting Muslim civilians. In the end, Western intervention brought about a peace settlement. Serbia reluctantly accepted Croatian and Bosnian independence but savagely repressed separatism in Kosovo in 1998–99, which once again prompted intervention and the bombing of Belgrade by Western air forces. Only intervention by Russia brought Milošević to accept the withdrawal of Serb forces.

Support your judgement

Read the sample exam question and two basic judgements below. Support the judgement that you agree with most strongly by adding a reason that justifies this judgement.

Tip: whichever option you choose, you will have to weigh up both sides of the argument. You could use phrases and words such as 'whereas' or 'although' in order to help the process of evaluation.

'The break-up of Yugoslavia was due to the collapse of the power and influence of the USSR.' How far do you agree?

The collapse of the power and influence of the USSR was the most important reason for the break-up of Yugoslavia.	The collapse of power and influence of the USSR alone could not have led to the break-up of Yugoslavia.

Recommended reading

As this is an area of historical debate and is part of the topics that could be set for the AS interpretation question, it is worth spending some time studying it in some depth, as this will enhance your understanding of the debates. Below is a list of suggested further reading on this topic.

- D. Williamson, *The Cold War 1941–95* (2015, Chapter 7)
- J. Laver, *The Eastern and Central European States 1945–1992* (1999)
- D. Mason, *Revolution in East-Central Europe* (1992)
- B. Magas, *Yugoslavia: Tracking the Break-up, 1980–1992* (1993)
- J. Laver, *Stagnation and Reform: the USSR 1964–91* (1997)
- M. McCauley, *Gorbachev* (1998)
- T. Ash, *We the People – The Revolution of 1990* (1990)

Exam focus

Below is a sample essay question and a model answer. Read them and the comments around the answer.

Assess the consequences in Eastern Europe, outside the former Soviet Union, of the overthrow of communist governments after 1989.

The end of communist rule had some common consequences for Eastern Europe outside the Soviet Union, but there were also some differences. In some countries greater unity resulted, for example when East Germany was united with West Germany. In the former Yugoslavia, the consequences were more in terms of disunity and subsequent violent struggle between the different parts of a country previously held together by communist rule. In most Eastern bloc countries there was a remarkably peaceful initial transition to more democratic and parliamentary rule, and only in Romania were former leaders killed. The principal consequences were: free elections and the re-emergence of a diversity of political parties; greater economic freedom and an end to economic controls; new relations with the West and freedom of travel and contacts. Of these the most significant was political change. There had been growing liberalisation before 1989 and the rigid separation of East and West had been reduced, but the Brezhnev Doctrine had ensured that there could be no real political freedom and diversity. Once that occurred after 1989, other changes became more rapid, so the most important consequence was political change.

One key consequence was the rise of nationalism and this was particularly seen in Yugoslavia. Possibly the greatest consequences for any single country took place in Yugoslavia, which had not been controlled by the USSR but whose communist government under Tito had been part of a non-aligned bloc. Tito's communist rule nevertheless held together very disparate elements in the Federal Republic of Yugoslavia and with the overthrow of communist governments in Eastern Europe and the death of Tito, Yugoslavia fell apart and nationalism became more dominant than communism. This had important consequences for Yugoslavia, which was the only country outside the old Soviet Union where civil war resulted after 1989. In Czechoslovakia there was a division between the Czech Republic and Slovakia, which was made peacefully. In Germany, the process was for reunification not further division. Countries like Romania and Bulgaria lacked the historic and religious divisions that affected Yugoslavia, which had been held together by communist rule. Slobodan Milošević represented Serb nationalism not communism and ended the self-governing status of Vojvodina and Kosovo. He also promoted the interests of Serb elements in Croatia and Bosnia. Similar nationalist elements in Croatia and Slovenia led to the break-up of the old Yugoslavia and to bitter conflict between Serbs, Croats and Bosnians and later between Serbs and ethnic Albanians in Kosovo. The situation was so serious that intervention by outside bodies occurred – something that did not result from the overthrow of communist governments in other parts of Eastern Europe. It was NATO intervention that brought about Serbian recognition of Croatian and Bosnian independence, but it took violent air campaigns against Serbia to bring a Serbian military withdrawal from Kosovo, an area still seen by many in Serbia as their territory. The violence brought about by the unrest in Romania in 1989 did not approach these levels, so it could be argued that the break-up of the state in Yugoslavia was the most dramatic and costly consequence, but because it was not typical of Eastern Europe outside the USSR it could perhaps be seen as not the most important.

The question does not ask for an account of the consequences but for an assessment, and the first paragraph offers a distinct view.

The answer draws a distinction between the consequences in different countries, but does not offer a series of descriptions. The section on Yugoslavia might have been more tightly linked to an overall consequence, however.

The answer discriminates between the different areas.

In terms of creating new states, the end of communism was highly significant and this, rather than civil war, might be seen as the most significant consequence. The reunification of Germany and the creation of the Czech Republic and the new states in Yugoslavia changed the political map of Central and south-east Europe. It seemed to suggest a much stronger Germany that might again dominate Europe and was the subject of much concern in some quarters in Britain and Poland. Reunification ended the armed border between East and West in Berlin and in Germany, and meant the withdrawal of allied troops from Germany. More than any one single change, the end of the Wall and German reunification indicated the end of the Cold War.

> This thematic approach leads the answer towards considering the theme of new countries.

However, not all countries saw the emergence of new states and boundaries, so as a consequence it might be argued that the political and economic liberalisation of Eastern Europe was more important. This affected more people and was a root cause of other changes in all the Eastern European satellites. The quick establishment of free elections and the emergence of centre and right parties as an alternative to communism dominated by Moscow was of great importance. It meant greater social, political and economic links with the West. It meant that the European Community expanded. There was also a link between political liberalism and a reduction of government controls and much greater economic freedom, which in turn gave rise to social changes. The consequences for the people in terms of changing the nature of lives, living standards, contacts with the wider world, and greater self-expression and choice in lifestyles and economic policy, was overwhelming. Not all was new and much had changed in economic and social terms before 1989, but not on the same level as after the overthrow of the communist governments. For Catholics in Poland, the ability to worship freely was of huge importance. In Romania the ending of the corrupt and dictatorial rule of the Ceausescus was of major emotional and political importance.

> This evaluation shows that the answer is addressing the question's wording: 'assess', rather than 'describe' or 'explain'.

Generally, political change was the key element and the most important consequence. Free elections did not always produce liberal solutions – Milošević's nationalism, for example – but they were central to change in many elements of life in Eastern Europe, as well as in its relations with the West. There were important social and economic consequences, but the political changes affected the whole nature of life in Eastern Europe and the relations of that region with the West.

> The closing section brings the answer back to the first paragraph and offers a distinct view about the relative importance of different consequences.

This is a strong answer that attempts to weigh the relative importance of different consequences and tries to use information rather than merely imparting it. The opening sets out a view, which is confirmed by the closing paragraph and there is weighing of consequences and not simply description.

Reverse engineering

Using the comments and the mark scheme on page 7, construct the plan that this answer seems to use and assess whether all the material is well linked to that plan. Rewrite any section that you think could be more closely linked to the plan.

Exam focus

Below is a sample exam-style question and a model answer. Read them and the comments around the answer.

Which did more to bring about the end of the USSR and the Cold War?

(i)   Gorbachev's policies in the USSR.

(ii)   The Russian war in Afghanistan.

Both these developments weakened the USSR and made it less able or willing to enforce the Brezhnev Doctrine and use force against unrest in its republics and satellite states. When the USSR broke up, the Cold War seemed to end as the USSR was no longer a superpower offering a threat to the West through a hostile and conflicting ideology. Gorbachev's internal policies indicated a big shift in political ideology but also led to some weakness. The war in Afghanistan eroded the confidence of Russian military and political leaders in their ability to control internal opposition and showed some of the weaknesses in the USSR that contributed to its break-up. Gorbachev's policies were the more significant in that they showed the greatest change in attitudes within the USSR since the Revolution, while the war in Afghanistan was more a contributory factor that influenced those changes.

> The two issues are linked to the question and a view is offered.

Control over the republics and the satellites had been maintained because of strict party discipline. The struggle for socialism was the dominant ideology, which justified economic, social and political controls. Gorbachev's reforms undermined the ideology itself by the policy of allowing greater economic freedom and initiative. There was almost an admission that the planning and state controls had not resulted in economic prosperity. The greater economic freedom of the West seemed now to be the more successful model, which undermined the whole basis of the USSR and the controls of the Comecon. Politically, greater accountability suggested that there had been weaknesses and problems with the communist state, and elections in 1989 saw the defeat of many in the party establishment and the rise of reformers like Yeltsin. Given these changes, it was logical for Gorbachev to seek greater détente with the West that lessened antagonism and reduced the high levels of defence spending. When challenges to the USSR came from within the satellite states, it would have been a major reversal of these liberal trends for Gorbachev to resist them with force. Without these key changes, changes would not have been attempted and fear of Soviet repression would have prevented change.

> There is a clear explanation of the links between the internal changes and the issue in the question.

The protracted and unsuccessful war in Afghanistan weakened the confidence of the leaders of the USSR in the ability of the armed forces to suppress revolts. The inability to defeat less well-equipped guerrilla forces was a blow to the prestige of the USSR and its armed forces. The resort to brutality weakened the USSR's reputation and also led to internal disturbances that threatened the loyalty of the Red Army. The unpopularity of the war contributed to the need for the new leaders of Russia to consider political change. The war became a symbol of the old order – repressive, yet ineffective.

> The war is considered in terms of its effects rather than in terms of what happened.

It is less important than the wider changes, however, because it was only one element leading to the changes that Gorbachev made, which in turn led to the change in attitude that led to accepting the end of control of the satellites and the Cold War. As well as the war, there was economic stagnation, an obvious falling behind the West in terms of economic development and military technology, and increasing restlessness in the Baltic states and the satellite countries. Without a new leader and a willingness to adopt new policies, these pressures would not have been enough to bring about change.

There is a clear judgement about relative importance, which puts the war into the context of other problems.

This is a clear and well-focused answer that deals with both issues in the question, even if there is rather more about the internal policies.

Balancing the answer

Look at the comments around this answer and the mark scheme on page 7 and identify the strengths of this response. Think about what might have been added to the analysis of the war to balance the answer more.

Exam focus

Below is a sample exam question for the AS-level interpretation question and a model answer. Read them and the comments around the answer.

The United States began to challenge the Soviet Union during the first half of the 1980s in a manner unprecedented since the early Cold War. That state soon exhausted itself and expired.

Source: J.L. Gaddis, We Now Know: Rethinking Cold War History

Evaluate the strengths and limitations of this interpretation, making reference to other interpretations that you have studied.

There is discussion between historians about whether US policy change and the pressure exerted by Reagan, both in terms of defence and a stronger political stance, were key or whether the better explanation lies in internal problems and changes within the USSR.

> This establishes the view within a broad debate – in the sense of different possible explanations.

This interpretation explains the collapse of the USSR and so the ending of the Cold War in terms of a change in US policy to challenging the USSR rather than relying on attempts to reduce nuclear weapons. This is a view that suggests it was Reagan's pressure by abandoning the Strategic Arms Limitation Talks and instead increasing the capacity of the USA in terms of defensive weapons systems – the so-called Star Wars initiatives and also improving missiles and offering a more direct threat to the USSR – that brought about the end of the Cold War.

Previously, the assumption had been that even if the USA had more weapons, any nuclear war would mean mutually assured destruction. So even if the USSR had fewer missiles, it would still be able to inflict huge damage and loss of life. This gave the USSR an advantage.

The Interpretation is correct that with the development of missile shields which were technically beyond the USSR the balance shifted towards the USA. This view is further supported as in order to maintain the balance of power, the USSR would need to spend huge sums on defence or rely on diplomacy and détente. In this climate it would be impossible to use huge force to suppress resistance within the USSR or its satellite states, with the danger of a more confident and aggressive USA. It is true that Gorbachev recognised this and was willing to revive détente as he understood that better relations with the West were vital, especially with the economic weakness of the USSR as the Interpretation implies. The Interpretation is correct to argue that in the past there had been a reluctance to confront the USSR as ongoing Strategic Arms Limitation Talks had shown. Kennedy had accepted the withdrawal of US missiles from Turkey and there had been no Western action taken over any of the USSR's suppression of unrest, for example in Czechoslovakia. It was true, as the Interpretation argues, that Reagan's harder line went back to the days of the late 1940s and offered a greater challenge to the USSR and used superior US technology and economic power. This, according to Gaddis in this extract, was decisive.

> This paragraph explains the view and offers support for it.

However, this view can be challenged by looking at the wider picture. The Interpretation does not consider the situation when military technology was more evenly matched, the Cold War showed little signs of ending, especially when the ideological position remained clear. The Interpretation fails to consider that there was a confident defence of the socialist ideology and assurance that the USSR and its satellites were pursuing the right road. The Interpretation does not acknowledge that by the 1980s the USSR's position had been eroded by the economic stagnation and the obvious imbalance between economic growth and living standards in East and West, which made a challenge from the USA more likely to succeed. When Gorbachev recognised this in his economic policies and when the Glasnost policy undermined the underlying ideology, it could be argued that the whole basis of the Cold War was being undermined. The defence issue merely revealed the limitations of the USSR, it did not create them as is suggested by the Interpretation. The movement for political change was a reflection of other problems in the USSR not, as the Interpretation suggests, simply meeting greater US assertion. Though the USA assisted the opposition in Afghanistan the war there was a result of inflexible Soviet policy and the poor performance due to internal weaknesses more than US aggression.

The view is then challenged but considers other factors.

Though US policy was linked to other factors, in itself it could not have ended the USSR and the Cold War. The USA was astute enough to realise that greater pressure would be effective; but the underlying weaknesses of the USSR were more significant than this extract suggests.

A clear view is offered.

This is a strong answer that would reach the higher levels. Some of the analysis could be more developed, for example about how the USA challenged the Soviet Union and how the USSR 'exhausted itself'. The view is put into the context of a possible debate, however, and the explanation is sustained and a judgement reached.

Reaching the very top

In the light of the comments above and the mark scheme, make a list of some additional material that could be used to strengthen the argument. Remember it does not have to be a perfect answer, only one that is a better fit with the descriptors.

Glossary

Annexation A term used to describe the establishment of political control by a state over other territories or countries.

Arms race A term used when rival countries or groups of countries build up their defences in case of attack, thereby accelerating each other's productions of weapons.

Atlantic Charter A statement made by Winston Churchill on 14 August 1941 for Britain and President Roosevelt for the USA on shared principles of democratic government as part of their goals for the post-war world before the USA had joined World War II.

Basic Law refers to the Constitution of the new West German state operative from 1949, the Federal Republic. After the centralised Nazi state, this law returned to a system that balanced the local governments of the individual states with the central authority of the President, Chancellor and two houses of parliament.

Benelux countries Belgium, the Netherlands and Luxemburg joined in a customs union in 1944 that was extended to wider political and cultural cooperation and a Benelux parliament in 1955. This was a step towards a wider European Union.

Big three The wartime leaders of the Allies – Stalin of Russia, Roosevelt of the USA and Churchill of Britain.

Bolshevik Revolution In October 1917 the Russian Bolshevik Party under Lenin seized power. The Bolsheviks were radical social democrats (socialists) who later became known as Communists.

Chernobyl A nuclear power station in Ukraine that suffered a severe and dangerous accident in 1986.

Cold War Hostility between the USSR and its allies and the Western democracies, which did not lead directly to open warfare.

Comecon An organisation based in Moscow to coordinate the economic policy of the USSR and its satellites states in Eastern Europe.

Cominform The political equivalent of Comecon; an organisation to strengthen and coordinate political links between the USSR and its Eastern European satellite states.

Comintern (or Third International, 1919–43) refers to the Communist International organisation set up in Moscow to coordinate the efforts of communists worldwide. In practice it was dominated by Russian Communist leaders.

Containment From 1947, US policy was to restrict the spread of communism.

Cuban adventure A term used to criticise the Russian leader Khrushchev for risking war by putting missiles on the island of Cuba, close to the USA, in 1962. This provoked a major crisis that brought the world close to nuclear war.

Deviationalist A term used in the communist world to condemn thinkers and leaders who stray from accepted interpretations of Marxist theory.

Dollar diplomacy The name given by the USSR to the way that the USA was supposed to use its financial and economic power to encourage good relations with other countries in order to promote US trade.

Draft dodging Avoiding responding to being called up for compulsory military service – called 'the draft' in the USA.

Fascism A term first used in Italy to describe a right-wing movement opposed to socialism and liberalism and promoting authoritarianism and nationalism.

Lend-Lease scheme On 11 March 1941 the US Congress passed an act to allow the US government to lend and lease supplies and military equipment to Britain and its allies for the duration of the war.

Morgenthau Plan A plan of the US secretary for the treasury in 1945 to demilitarise post-war Germany and to reduce its industry to prevent it from waging future war.

Mujahedeen Armed Islamic groups who opposed Russian rule in Afghanistan and were supported by the USA in the 1980s.

Mutually Assured Destruction This referred to the view that any use of nuclear weapons might lead to total destruction of the countries who used them and therefore possession of weapons was a deterrent.

Non-Aligned Movement A movement of states that did not want to ally with either the non-communist West or the communist countries, but to stay away from ideological conflict. Its leading proponents were Tito of Yugoslavia and Nehru of India.

Popular Front The name given to coalitions of left-wing groups in Europe encouraged by

Stalin in order to win elections. This resulted in left-wing governments in Spain and France. In Spain civil war resulted, while France was deeply divided.

Prague Spring The emergence in 1968 of a more liberal regime in Czechoslovakia that was ended by the Soviet invasion.

Proletariat The name given in Marxist theory to the industrial working class who are destined to take over the state in industrial capitalist nations.

Proxy war Communist regimes and the West backed rival groups in other countries who fought notionally for the ideas of their backers.

Red Scare Anti-communist anxiety and hysteria in the USA, with fears that communism would subvert or control US society.

Representative government The name given to government in which the people elect those who rule them and represent them in parliamentary assemblies.

Salami tactics The name given to the method of gradual takeover by the USSR of Eastern European states by eliminating opposition – 'sliced' like the cutting of a salami sausage.

SED The initials of the Socialist Unity Party of Germany after the USSR forced the merger of the Communist Party (KPD) and the Socialist Party (SPD) in East Germany in April 1946. Under Soviet domination, it ruled East Germany from 1949 to 1989.

Soviet bloc The name given to the communist countries that were dominated by the USSR after World War II.

Sudetenland The name given to the northern border region of the new state of Czechoslovakia, which consisted mostly of German speakers. Their demands for autonomy, encouraged by Hitler in the 1930s, led to a crisis in 1938 and the region was made part of Germany until 1945.

Totalitarianism A system of government where the rulers control the totality of people's lives and mould their beliefs and private lives in the service of the state.

Union of Soviet Socialist Republics (USSR) The former Russian Empire under Soviet rule was a federation of socialist republics formed in 1922. The different republics had nominal self-government but in practice were dominated by the Communist Party and its leaders in Moscow.

Vietnam War From 1955 to 1975 there was a civil war between communist forces backed by North Vietnam and their opponents for control of South Vietnam. This escalated with US involvement, particularly from the early 1960s to the US withdrawal in 1973, after which the communists won.

Profiles

Konrad Adenauer (1876–1967) was a conservative Catholic lawyer who became Mayor of Cologne in 1917. Imprisoned in 1944 by the Nazis whom he opposed, he helped found the Christian Democratic Union (CDU) party in 1945 and was Chancellor of the Federal Republic 1949–63. He established a prosperous and politically stable nation and remained hostile to the Communist bloc.

Willy Brandt (1913–92) was a dedicated socialist who opposed the Nazis and fled abroad in 1933. He became Mayor of West Berlin in 1957 and chairman of the Socialist SPD in 1964. As foreign minister in 1966 and then as Chancellor 1969–74 he pursued better relations with the East (Ostpolitik). He resigned in 1974 over a spy scandal.

Leonid Brezhnev (1906–82) was the son of a steelworker who rose in the Communist Party under Stalin, becoming party leader in Moldova. He entered the Politburo but his fortunes declined under Khrushchev and he did not return to central government until 1964. He was the dominant influence in the 1970s but under his rule the USSR stagnated.

Nicolae Ceausescu (1918–89) came from a Romanian peasant family and was an active communist, arrested and imprisoned many times. In 1947 he joined the Communist government and was leader of the party from 1965. Increasingly corrupt and repressive, his unpopularity was such that in 1989 he and his wife Elena were killed after popular risings overthrew the regime.

Winston Churchill (1874–1965) held senior offices from 1908 to 1929, first as a Liberal and then a Conservative, before his opposition to self-government for India and calls for re-armament led to his political isolation. He returned to office in 1939 and was prime minister 1940–45. He was one of the 'big three' world leaders, with Roosevelt and Stalin, and made the term 'iron curtain' famous. He was prime minister again 1951–55 but suffered from declining health.

Alexander Dubček (1921–92) was a communist from Slovakia who had resisted German occupation of Czechoslovakia. He introduced economic reforms in 1965 and was seen as a liberaliser. He became party secretary in 1968 and introduced more democracy, but could not persuade the USSR of his loyalty. He was taken to Moscow after the Soviet invasion in August 1968, forced to resign in 1969 and take a lowly job as a clerk.

Wladyslaw Gomułka (1905–82) rose in the Polish trade union movement and resisted German occupation 1940–45. He was made vice president of Poland in 1945 but fell out of favour with Stalin and was in danger of execution. He was installed by Khrushchev as first secretary to appease discontent in Poland in 1956. He resigned in 1970 after economic problems caused a renewal of discontent.

Mikhail Gorbachev (1931–) rose though the Communist Party as an agricultural expert in the 1970s and in 1985 became at 54 the youngest general secretary in the history of the USSR. His reforms and diplomacy changed the nature of the USSR and its relationship with the West and led to the end of the Cold War, but they provoked opposition and a coup in 1991. He never aimed to destroy the Communist Party or the USSR but his policies brought about both of these developments.

Janos Kadar (1912–89) was a prominent Communist Party leader in Hungary before World War II. After the Hungarian rising he was installed as leader by the USSR. He made few political concessions but ensured better living standards and introduced what was known as 'Goulash Communism' to ensure less discontent by greater prosperity. He remained in power until 1988.

John F. Kennedy (1917–63) was from a wealthy and influential family. After serving in the navy in World War II, he entered Congress as a Democrat and was elected president in 1960, defeating Richard Nixon. He dealt successfully with the Cuban Missile Crisis in 1962 but his internal reforms were often blocked by Congress. An inspiration to many, he was assassinated in 1963.

Nikita Khrushchev (1894–1971) was active in the Bolshevik Party and a loyal supporter of Stalin, assisting with key policies and purges. Active in organising guerrilla resistance in the Ukraine in World War II, he was one of a group who ruled the USSR after 1953, coming to be dominant by 1956 when he condemned Stalin's policies. His own policies had mixed success and he brought the world close to war by putting missiles on Cuba in 1962. He was ousted from power by colleagues in 1964.

Karl Marx (1818–83) was a radical German journalist. He was exiled from Germany after the revolutions of 1848 and wrote his influential study of the inevitable fall of capitalism while living in London, where he is buried. His most famous works are *The Communist Manifesto* and *Das Kapital*. He tried to unite those who worked for socialism in an international organisation. He expected a workers' revolution to occur in economically advanced countries, not in Russia or China.

Slobodan Milošević (1941–2006) was the son of a Serbian priest who became a manager and banker before taking a leading role in politics. An ardent Serb nationalist, he was president of Serbia 1989–97 then president of Yugoslavia. He fought brutal wars to try to prevent Croatia and Bosnia becoming independent and then agreed to a peace in 1995 but used force in Kosovo until deterred by NATO bombing. He lost power in 2000 and was then tried as a war criminal.

Franklin D. Roosevelt (1882–1945) was elected Democratic president in 1932 and his New Deal policies offered relief, recovery and reform to the Depression-hit USA. He led the USA in World War II but died in April 1945 before seeing final victory. He was highly influential in forming post-war Europe.

Josef Stalin (1878–1953) was born in Georgia as Josef Djugashvili. Known as 'Stalin' after he became a Bolshevik, he was a leading party member who had full command of the party and the USSR by 1928. He transformed the economy of the USSR by collectivisation and industrialisation and maintained a reign of terror to ensure he remained in power. This was imposed on Eastern Europe after the USSR's victory in World War II.

Tito (Josip Broz, 1892–1980) was a Croatian communist who took part in the Russian Revolution in 1917 and worked in Yugoslavia for revolution. Arrested and imprisoned, he fled to the USSR and fought in the Spanish Civil War. When Nazi Germany occupied Yugoslavia, he fought for freedom and was aided by the USA and Britain. He became premier in 1945. He resisted the influence of Stalin, and Yugoslavia – the federation he created – remained independent under his rule.

Harry S Truman (1884–1972) was a previously little-known Democratic politician who as vice president took over the presidency in 1945 when Roosevelt died. He took the decision to use atomic weapons against Japan and adopted a harder line with the USSR. This led to the policy of containment. He led the USA into the Korean War in 1950.

Boris Yeltsin (1931–2007) was a Communist politician from Sverdlovsk who supported change in the 1980s but enjoyed poor relations with Gorbachev after 1985. He was the only person to resign from the Politburo. He was a popular mayor of Moscow and was influential in defeating the coup against Gorbachev in that city in 1991. He went on to lead the Russian Federation but faced considerable problems, which led him to rely too much on drinking.

Timeline

1917	October	Bolshevik Revolution in Russia
1939	August	Nazi–Soviet Pact
1939–40		Winter War with Finland
1941		German invasion of Russia
1942		German attack on Stalingrad
1943	February	Failure of Germany at Stalingrad
	November	Stalin, Churchill and Roosevelt meet at Tehran
1944		Russia fails to support Warsaw Uprising
1944	June	D-Day sees start of second front
		Greek Civil War
		Soviet forces control Bulgaria through Allied Control Council
	October	Churchill and Stalin agree Percentages Agreement on Eastern Europe
1945	February	Yalta Conference
	April	Death of Roosevelt
	June	Soviet forces set up Provisional Government in Poland
	July–August	Potsdam Conference
	August	USA drops atom bombs on Hiroshima and Nagasaki
		Russia supports coup in Romania
1946	March	Churchill's Iron Curtain speech
1947		Policy of containment starts
		Bizonia created
	June	Marshall Plan
	September	Cominform established
1948	February	Communist coup in Czechoslovakia
		Expulsion of Yugoslavia from Cominform
1948–49		Berlin blockade
1949		Comecon established
	April	Trizonia created
		NATO established
		Basic Law establishes West Germany
		Communist Party takes power in China
	August	USSR detonates atom bomb
1950–53		Korean War
1953		Execution of Julius and Ethel Rosenberg
		Death of Stalin
		Unrest in East Germany
1954		USA produces hydrogen bomb
1955		Warsaw Pact signed
		West Germany joins NATO
		Hallstein Doctrine
1956		Suez Crisis
		Hungarian rising
1957		Russia tests ICBM
	October	Sputnik launched
1961		Berlin Wall built
1962	February	First American in space
	October	Cuban Missile Crisis
1963	August	The Partial Test Ban Treaty
1968	January	Dubcek into power in Czechoslovakia
		Prague Spring
	August	Soviet forces invade Czechoslovakia
		Brezhnev Doctrine
1969	July	USA lands man on the moon
		Ostpolitik pursued by West German Chancellor Willy Brandt
1970	August	Moscow Treaty signed by Brandt and Brezhnev
1972	December	Basic Treaty between West and East Germany
		President Nixon visits China
		SALT Treaty
1979		SALT II signed in Vienna by Carter and Brezhnev
	December	USSR invades Afghanistan
1980		Ronald Reagan becomes US President
1985		Gorbachev becomes General Secretary of USSR Communist Party
1989		Fall of Berlin Wall
1990		Reunification of Germany
1991		End of USSR
		Slovenia and Croatia declared independence

Answers

1 The origins of the Cold War to 1945

Page 9, Turning assertion into argument

The West feared the spread of communism because **it was hostile to its aims and ideology.**

However, it was Stalin's alliance with Hitler that caused most concern, because **it appeared to show that communism had more in common with fascism.**

Although there were also concerns in the West about Stalin's domestic policies because **of the rapid economic growth and the repression of the people.**

Page 11, Support your judgement

The wartime alliance was a success because **it led to the defeat of Germany.**

The wartime alliance was a failure because **it was short-lived and created further tensions between East and West.**

Page 13, Develop the detail

Churchill had a number of aims at Tehran**, including agreeing the post-war division of Germany and establishing the UN**. He had some limited success, but there were more failures **over Poland**, most notably over the second front and his failure to secure agreement over his preferred policy**, which was to invade Europe from the Balkans**. Churchill was also concerned about the increasing presence of the Soviets in the East of Europe, particularly given the reason why Britain had gone to war**, which had been to defend Poland**. Churchill was also concerned about his relationship with Roosevelt and the improvement in relations between Roosevelt and Stalin**, who had a number of secret meetings**.

Page 15, Challenge the historian

1 What is the view of the interpretation?

Tensions between the USA and USSR were inevitable.

2 What knowledge of your own do you have that supports the interpretation?

They had different political and economic systems.

3 What knowledge of your own do you have that challenges the interpretation?

Relations between Stalin and Roosevelt were good.

Page 17, Support your judgement

Overall, the most serious consequence of the liberation of Eastern Europe was the political domination of the USSR **as it now had influence or political control in all of Eastern Europe except Greece.** However, it was not the political domination of the USSR but the annexation of territory that was the most important consequence of the liberation of Eastern Europe **as Russian troops now occupied large amounts of Eastern Europe and could overrun the West.**

Page 19, Develop the detail

The two leaders, **Roosevelt and Churchill,** were very close in the early years of the war. Churchill travelled to meet Roosevelt **in Canada** and signed an agreement**, the Atlantic Charter,** with him, even though it was a threat to the British Empire **because of its democratic principles**. Churchill was able to gain Roosevelt's support for the war and initially for his strategy **of focusing on the Mediterranean and North Africa.** However, the relationship did change because of the direction of British attacks**, which appeared to be designed to protect the British Empire**. Roosevelt believed that this did not benefit US needs **in terms of trade** or beliefs **in freedom**. Eventually, Roosevelt was able to force his views on Churchill **and force him to agree to open a second front in France**.

2 The development of the Cold War 1946–1955

Page 27, Support or challenge?

	Support	Challenge
The term 'iron curtain' became widely used to describe the Soviet bloc.		✗
Stalin argued that the Soviet Union had a right to ensure its own security after the losses of the war.		✗
US policy did not change after the speech.	✗	
Many considered Churchill's speech to be irresponsible.		✗
The views of foreign policy experts, such as George Kennan, were more important.	✗	
The speech did not change US views about the Soviet Union, but simply confirmed them.	✗	
Truman did not immediately give his support to Churchill's views.	✗	
Some of Churchill's claims, such as Berlin being under Russian control, were inaccurate.	✗	
The speech encouraged anti-Russian sentiment.		✗

Page 29, Develop the detail

The Soviet Union used a range of methods and tactics, **most notably salami tactics,** to gain control in Eastern Europe. In many states, **such as the Soviet zone in Germany,** non-communist parties were merged with the communists, who soon dominated the new party, **the Socialist Unity Party**. This eventually led to the situation whereby the communists were the only party allowed to stand for election, **as in Hungary and Bulgaria,** or if opposition was allowed it faced intimidation, **as in Poland**. The Soviets also used the army in some countries **such as Bulgaria and Czechoslovakia** to help impose their domination, while in other states **such as Hungary** the opposition was either arrested or, in some places **such as Poland**, resigned in protest.

Page 31, Turning assertion into argument

The US economy gained substantially from the policy of containment because **the aid given was used to purchase US goods.**

Though important to the USA, containment was beneficial to the West because **it was too weak to resist communism without support.**

Most importantly, it created hostility in the Communist bloc because **they believed its aim was to destroy communism.**

Page 33, Delete as applicable

The establishment of Cominform and Comecon was **important** in increasing Soviet control over Eastern Europe. Marshall Aid **threatened** Soviet control and would have **required** trade with the West. Comecon also **increased** the USSR's control of its satellite states. Comecon and Cominform were also part of a wider programme of **resisting** US policies in Europe, and this led to the USSR **strengthening** its control over East Berlin. The policy also resulted in the USSR **strengthening** its control over Czechoslovakia.

Page 35, Support or challenge?

	Support	Challenge
Britain and the USA merged their zones to form Bizonia.		✗
The USSR wanted heavy reparations from the Western zone.	✗	
Bizonia ceased reparation payments to Russia and developed an industrial base in its zones.		✗
The USSR encouraged merger between the communists and SPD.	✗	
The USSR did not want a developed industrial region under Western control.	✗	
The Western powers agreed to the formation of a new West German state.		✗
The West introduced a new currency into its zone without consulting the USSR.		✗
The USSR imposed a blockade on road and rail links to West Berlin.	✗	
The USSR introduced its own currency for the East.	✗	

Page 35, Turning assertion into argument

The introduction of a new currency into the Western zone ended any hope of a united Germany because **the Soviet Union was not consulted and it was a further move towards a West German state.**

Though important, the introduction of a new currency into the Western zone was not the most important reason because **there were already tensions over the creation of Bizonia.**

More important was the attitude of the Soviet Union to the industrialisation of the Western zone because **it did not want the Western zone's economy to develop.**

Page 37, Turning assertion into argument

The SED supported national unity because **this was the view of the Russian Communist Party.**

However, in reality it feared West Germany's economic power because **it would be richer and more powerful than that of the East.**

The SED was also concerned that West Germany would join NATO because **it would threaten the security of the East.**

Page 39, Develop the detail

There were many reasons for the creation and expansion of NATO in the years to 1955**, including mutual defence against Soviet aggression, but also political reasons**. There were no longer fears about Germany but initially talks began because of events that had taken place in Europe in 1948 **with the Communist seizure of power in Czechoslovakia**. The process was given greater urgency because of developments in Russia **with the development of an atomic bomb** and China **where the communists had been victorious** and the outbreak of war in 1950 **in Korea**. NATO was created not only for mutual defence, but also for ideological reasons **to uphold freedom, common heritage and civilisation**.

3 The Cold War 1956–1984

Page 45, Spot the mistake

The answer describes events and there is no argument about how or whether the events in Poland and Hungary had an impact on the Cold War.

Page 45, Turning assertion into argument

The events in Poland were a cause of unrest in Hungary in 1956 because **they encouraged similar resistance to Stalinist policies in Hungary as it appeared Poland had been able to install a more liberal leader.**

However, the Stalinist policies of Rakosi were more significant because **they were repressive and led to calls for his removal.**

In the short term, a major reason for the unrest was the actions of the police because **they fired on protestors, which encouraged workers to join students and intellectuals in protesting.**

Page 47, Complete the paragraph

The Soviet Union initially expressed concern about the anti-Russian propaganda that emanated from Czechoslovakia. At first the Soviet Union simply put pressure on the Czech leader, Dubcek, to control criticisms and this was given added force by the extension of Warsaw Pact manoeuvres in the country, which should have left the Czech leader in no doubt as to what could follow. This meant that when the Soviet Union became fearful of the break-up of the Eastern bloc, following the visit of both the Yugoslav and Romanian leaders to Czechoslovakia, it was easy for them to take action. **The Soviet response was effective as military force soon destroyed Czech resistance, while the Soviet government was able to force the Czech leadership to abandon reforms thus quickly ending any sustainable opposition.**

Page 47, Develop the detail

The events in Czechoslovakia in 1968 were a serious threat to the Soviet Union's control in Eastern Europe **as they would have led to greater democracy**. Firstly, there were concerns about the Czechs developing economic links **with West Germany**, which could be a threat to the economic stability of the East. There were also concerns that freedom of expression would lead to critical ideas spreading**, particularly if individuals were allowed to have a greater input into decision making**. It appeared as if such events were part of wider criticism of Moscow**, particularly after knowledge of the crimes and repression under Stalin became known**. Although the sending of troops to suppress unrest might damage relations with the West, **particularly détente, and lead to a strengthening of NATO,** there were concerns that unrest could spread **to other Eastern bloc states and weaken Moscow's control** and therefore a variety of pressures were put on the Czech leaders, **with them taken to Moscow and forced to abandon reforms,** suggesting that the Soviet Union did consider the events a serious threat.

Page 51, Develop the detail

The economic situation in the East was particularly bad **with the loss of skilled labour** and was not helped by Soviet policies**, which had restrictive controls and wasteful production**. On the other hand, the situation in the West was much better **as the West had experienced an economic miracle with a developed capitalist consumer economy and reindustrialisation and trade links with the Common Market and US aid,** and it could be used to show the failings of communism. This development also encouraged emigration from the East to the West**, with 3.5 million leaving by 1961,** and this also had a serious impact on the East, particularly as numbers had been rising **and many of those who left were skilled workers**. It was essential for Russia to show other powers**, particularly China,** that its policies worked, but this was not happening. The East Germans were also concerned by the developments **as they faced shortages and had an old-fashioned economy** and were pleased when Russia approved the building of the Wall.

Page 53, Turning assertion into argument

The arms race increased tensions between the East and West because **a successful missile strike could prevent the launch of a counter-attack.**

However, in many instances it also encouraged peace movements and summits because **both sides were concerned that it could escalate into nuclear war.**

But, on many occasions these were not very effective because **both sides were suspicious of the other.**

Page 55, Turning assertion into argument

The Space Race was a triumph for US technology because **its initiative led to 1957–58 being declared International Geophysical Year, with 67 countries contributing to research and the USA planning a satellite.**

However, in the early years it was the Russians who were triumphant because **their technology was more advanced and they were able to launch satellites before the USA.**

Moreover, the US achievements were also seen as limited because **capitalism had not produced the levels of superiority that they expected.**

Page 57, Support or challenge?

	Support	Challenge
The USSR's relations with China were worsening, leading to border clashes.		✗
The USA was involved in a costly war in Vietnam.		✗
Nixon visited China in 1972.	✗	
The rising oil prices made a reduction in arms spending a sensible policy.		✗
US–China relations improved following Nixon's visit, leaving the USSR more isolated.	✗	
The leadership in both the USA and USSR was more pragmatic and put national interest first.		✗
There had been fears of a nuclear war since the Cuban Missile Crisis.		✗
The USSR hoped that by improving relations with the USA it would prevent a Chinese–American alliance.	✗	

Page 57, Delete as applicable

The policy of détente was **a failure** by the end of the 1970s. Talks to reduce nuclear weapons took place between the two countries and treaties were signed **soon after** the talks. Contacts between the two countries also **increased** and this development was **helped** by a joint space programme. The treaties signed by the two nations **were far reaching** and **left vulnerable** much of each country. SALT II, signed in 1979, was a further **disappointment** as it reduced missile launchers and warheads and the US Senate **refused to sign** the treaty.

Page 61, Turning assertion into argument

It could be argued that the elections of Reagan and Thatcher were important because **they were hostile to communism and determined to oppose it.**

Their position was further strengthened by their economic and technological resources because **they were far superior to those of the USSR and they could afford to use them to develop new weapons and defence programmes.**

On the other hand, there were fears over developments in Afghanistan because **it created fears of Russian expansion towards the Persian Gulf and the supplies of oil.**

4 The end of the Cold War 1984–1995

Page 65, Develop the detail

The USSR and Eastern Europe faced many social and economic problems **with the quality of the goods it produced, poor motivation among the workforce and problems of motivation, absenteeism and alcoholism.** These problems weakened the position of the Communist Party. The major problem was the weakness of the communist system**, as planning objectives were unrealistic.** There were many problems and these had spread to Eastern Europe, where they created an even greater problem **because they were closer to the more successful capitalist economies.** However, the situation had not always been as bad, particularly when the West was suffering from problems after 1973 and the USSR was more stable **and had experienced growth compared with the West, which had suffered from rising oil prices and rapid inflation.**

Page 67, Support or challenge?

	Support	Challenge
The USA increased its military spending, which put pressure on the USSR.	✗	
Gorbachev was able to achieve the total withdrawal of medium-range missiles from Europe.		✗
Economic growth in Russia was declining.		✗
The USA had developed the SDI.	✗	
The USSR faced a shortage of oil.		✗
The West was able to exert pressure on communist influence in Nicaragua and Grenada.		✗
The difficulties created for the USSR by the war in Afghanistan.		✗
The new arms technology was very expensive.	✗	
There were problems in the USSR's republics and satellites.		✗

Page 67, Challenge the historian

1 What is the view of the interpretation?

It ended because of Soviet economic problems.

2 What knowledge of your own do you have that supports the interpretation?

The goods produced were of poor quality and the workforce was poorly motivated.

3 What knowledge of your own do you have that challenges the interpretation?

The Soviet economy had performed better than that of the West before the 1980s because of oil prices and inflation.

Page 69, Turning assertion into argument

The policies of perestroika and glasnost were the most important reasons for the ending of the Cold War because **they weakened communist control, which led to a weakening of the Soviet Empire, and the leadership wanted change.**

However, the military power of the USA was important because **the USSR was unable to keep pace with or afford the developments.**

Yet it was not as important because **Gorbachev did increase the number of missiles in Eastern Europe and get the withdrawal of medium-range missiles from Europe.**

Page 71, Develop the detail

The invasion and war in Afghanistan had a serious impact on both the Soviet military, **whose reputation and confidence was damaged by its inability to defeat a guerrilla force,** and the economy, **which could not meet the heavier defence spending and was having to import more oil and wheat**. In previous conflicts the Soviets had been able to secure a quick victory, but this did not happen in Afghanistan **and some 38,000 were either killed or wounded**. This had a serious impact on the attitude of the Soviet military, **who resorted to acts of brutality,** as it showed that the army was weak and had an impact on its attitude towards the Eastern bloc, **suggesting it would be unable to maintain control over it**. The war also caused resentment within the Soviet Union and this was added to by the press, **whose reports led to discontent and a demand for political change**.

Page 71, Use your own knowledge to support or contradict

● Summary:

The war showed the weakness of the military, encouraging the republics to demand independence.

● Agree with the interpretation:

There were mutinies within the army.

● Contradict the interpretation:

The Russian forces were willing to be brutal to defeat the Afghan forces and could do the same elsewhere.

Page 73, Support your judgement

Reforming leaders were important in bringing about political change in Eastern Europe because **in states such as Hungary and Bulgaria they were willing to share power. However,** popular support for change was the most important factor in bringing about political change because **of the large numbers who took to the streets, which forced leaders to reform as in Germany, Hungary and Poland.**

Page 75, Eliminate irrelevance

Gorbachev had introduced significant changes since 1989 and these had created opposition from many conservative elements within the Communist Party. ~~Gorbachev had introduced polices of perestroika and glasnost, which restricted the economy and relaxed central control, allowing more economic freedom and openness to discuss economic and political issues.~~ There was considerable opposition to the policies of perestroika and glasnost among important and powerful elements within the Communist Party, such as the army and KGB. It was the strength of support in the army that allowed it to seize the TV and radio stations in Moscow. The army was also able to seize Gorbachev while he was on holiday in Crimea and was cut off from all links with Moscow. ~~If this coup had succeeded, it is likely that all the improvement in relations between the East and West that had been achieved by Gorbachev would have ended and the Cold War restarted.~~ However, the actions of Boris Yeltsin ensured that, despite the apparent strength of the plotters, the coup failed.

Page 75, Challenge the historian

1 What is the view of the interpretation?

It was defeated due to a range of factors.

2 What knowledge of your own do you have that supports the interpretation?

The army ultimately withdrew, large numbers protested and the plotters did not have a clear plan.

3 What knowledge of your own do you have that challenges the interpretation?

The actions of Yeltsin, making an emotional appeal and jumping on a tank, also played a significant role in its defeat.

Page 77, Develop the detail

The reunification of Germany was very significant. The division of Germany had kept it weak, **unable to change the 1945 boundaries,** and prevented its dominance **in Central Europe**, which it had exerted in the past **in both 1914 and 1939**. Politically, the division had prevented the rise of extremism, **particularly right-wing nationalism,** and resulted in democracy **– parliamentary in the West and social democracy in the East**. Prussian power **based on militarism, its army and monarchy** had also been prevented by the division from re-emerging. The two states had also been members of various organisations, **such as NATO, the EU and Warsaw Pact,** which had prevented them from pursuing policies of revenge. It was possible that all of these issues could re-emerge now that the country was reunited, **with the Poles frightened about their western border and Thatcher and Mitterrand both expressing concern and Israel completely opposed.**